Praise for

Challenging Coaching

"This is a terrific book that should provoke and challenge coaches to 'up their game' and thus provide more value to individuals and also, vitally, to their organizations. Read it and I believe you will improve your coaching."
Graham Alexander, Founder of The Alexander Corporation, originator of the GROW Model, and author of SuperCoaching *and* Tales from the Top

"Right on target. This book is so practical it reads like a Haynes manual for a style of coaching and leadership based on real human values rather than abstract processes. Notions such as courageous goal setting, feedback as the 'loving boot,' the 'player coach,' and the 'R' word (responsibility!) particularly rang true for me. These are powerful ideas consistent with my own belief that leadership takes place on the pitch not on the side-lines. I loved it."
Andrew Gould, CEO UK, Jones Lang LaSalle

"This is a book that is at the same time inspiring and transformational. Inspiring because it reinforces the motivational aspects of coaching and transformational because it progresses the discipline in light of today's business environment. I recommend this book to all coaches who wish to challenge conventional coaching techniques."
Julian Wais, Director of Investor Relations, Cobham plc

"Not just for the coaches, this book is critical reading for any business leader seeking to take an honest and challenging approach to developing their people, as well as anyone seeking to add robustness and realism to their business relationships."
Scott Sunderman, Managing Director, Healix Group

"I have experience of working with both John and Ian and have found their FACTS method of coaching both energizes individuals and ensures alignment with company goals. Any coach who truly wants to add value to the bottom line of their clients should take note of the key messages in this book and not be afraid to challenge the established 'comfortable norms,' particularly in these uncertain and increasingly competitive economic times."
Yvonne Spalding, Director, Group Professional Services, SSP Ltd

"*Challenging Coaching* is practical, honest, and relevant—especially for those coaching within more performance driven cultures. The authors write in a refreshingly clear and straightforward style. The insightful exercises, in particular, can be used as a self-development tool to help coaches to raise their game further, or alternatively, within coach supervision."
Katherine Tulpa, CEO, Association for Coaching

"A gem of a book achieving the rare mix of challenging conventional concepts whilst offering very practical advice. This is for business leaders, scholars, and students who believe in mindfulness, impact, and performance. If you want to change the conversations in your business then 'face the FACTS' as the authors suggest."
Brigitte Nicoulaud, Director of MBA Programmes, Aston Business School

Challenging Coaching

Going beyond traditional coaching

to face the FACTS

John Blakey and Ian Day

NICHOLAS BREALEY
PUBLISHING

London • Boston

First published in the UK in 2012 by Nicholas Brealey Publishing
An imprint of John Murray Press

An Hachette company

3

Copyright © John Blakey and Ian Day, 2012
English translation © Ross Benjamin, 2011

The right of John Blakey and Ian Day to be identified as the Authors of the Work has been
asserted by them in accordance with the Copyright, Designs and Patents Act 1988.

FACTS coaching copyright © 2009. All rights reserved.

British Library Cataloguing-in-Publication Data
A CIP catalogue record for this book is available from the British Library

ISBN 978-1-90483-839-5
eBook ISBN 978-1-85788-950-5

Printed and bound by Clays Ltd, St Ives plc

John Murray Press policy is to use papers that are natural, renewable and
recyclable products and made from wood grown in sustainable forests. The logging
and manufacturing processes are expected to conform to the environmental
regulations of the country of origin.

Nicholas Brealey Publishing
John Murray Press
Carmelite House
50 Victoria Embankment
London, EC4Y 0DZ, UK
Tel: 020 3122 6000

Nicholas Brealey Publishing
Hachette Book Group
Market Place Center, 53 State Street
Boston, MA 02109, USA
Tel: (617) 523 3801

www.nicholasbrealey.com
www.challengingcoaching.co.uk

Contents

Contents

Foreword
by Sir John Whitmore

This is a book that questions the role and responsibility of coaches generally. Its title suggests that executive coaches could be more courageous and do more to warn about, help, or even avert the challenges faced by their clients. Through its contents, John and Ian aim to upgrade the skills and thereby the confidence of existing coaches—for all too often we shrink from challenging our clients when in fact a challenge would be both appreciated and beneficial.

Understanding that the roots of business coaching lie in the progressive psychology of Carl Rogers and Gerard Egan and are therapy based is important if one wants to fully understand the impact of workplace coaching and also to recognize the limitations of this heritage; that is, not all of the person-centered counseling approaches are appropriate or effective in a corporate environment. Similarly, the existing forms of sports coaching have a lot to contribute to effective coaching in the workplace, yet some of these are preoccupied with instruction on technique, which becomes less effective when placed into a political and dynamic business landscape. It is important to recognize that there are unique features of the business coaching challenge that require new and tailored approaches and it is on this specific agenda that this book focuses its attention.

Importantly, the book challenges coaches too by giving them permission to break some of the "golden rules" of coaching, for example the principle of staying on the coachee's agenda exclusively. It actually encourages breaking this rule and I wholeheartedly agree with this. A coach's task and responsibility are to benefit not only the coachee, but also the client company and all of society too.

John and Ian briefly reference several models of coaching such as the GROW model, which is sometimes attributed to me, before focusing on their FACTS approach, the theme of this book. They give guidance about the more sophisticated aspects of coaching and the kinds of questions good coaches can usefully ask, providing illustrative examples. The FACTS model is clear, well laid out, and easy to grasp. Hopefully it will be a road map for coaches to use to venture into the less-charted territories of conventional executive coaching.

My personal reflections on the various components of the FACTS approach are as follows.

Feedback: Coaching has generally been perceived as a bit "soft," with many people asking nice questions in a nice sort of way. Of course, this approach is often very appropriate, but sometimes it is not. An example from my own experience may help to illustrate this point. I asked a coachee of mine: "How committed on a scale of 0 to 10 are you to taking this action?" He instantly replied: "Oh, I would be 9 out of 10 for sure." Yet, I heard something in the tone of his voice that led me to doubt his conviction. I paused for 30 seconds and then said: "That's rubbish, I don't believe you." My coachee also then paused for 30 seconds and replied: "You're absolutely right—I was just trying to get you off my back." This example shows that sometimes challenging feedback is necessary for change to happen. When people say to me: "That isn't coaching," I reply: "Anything that is appropriate in the moment to help a person move from *A* to *B* is coaching."

Accountability: I prefer the word responsibility to accountability, since I believe it is more human, yet these words are interchangeable in the context of this book. The key point here is that as coaches we are not responsible just to ourselves but to everyone else in the organizational system in which we are operating. To use an analogy from soccer, just because the goalkeeper's specialist function is to keep the ball out of the net, that does not mean he is not also responsible for the goals of the wider team (no pun intended). If he or she sees issues or risks that are affecting the wider team, then he or she has a responsibility to raise these and do something about them. The same is true for coaches and for leaders who have responsibility for the bigger picture in which they operate.

Courageous goals: I call this the dream. What is your dream? A dream serves as an incredibly valuable purpose, even if it is not achieved. Let me give you an example that is close to home. My son, Jason, was watching the men's Wimbledon final on television when he was a small boy. The commentator was bemoaning the fact that not since 1936 had an Englishman lifted the trophy. My son suddenly exclaimed: "Oh my God, what if I were the next Englishman to win at Wimbledon?" This became his dream—it motivated and inspired him as he pursued his tennis career over the coming years. As a 12 year old he played for his county and beat the then unknown Maria Sharapova; this would not have happened without the power of his dream. Unfortunately his career was cut short by illness and the dream was not achieved, but it had served him well every day it was kept alive. As John and Ian would say: "Dream, share, start..."

Tension: While I agree with John and Ian about the constructive role of tension in the coaching relationship, I must add a word of caution. Tension is a very individual dynamic: some people thrive on high levels of tension, for others it can be damaging. The key is to know the person in front of you and to carry out the dynamic calibration that John and Ian propose in order to make sure that the level of tension is optimized. We have a duty of care to the people we work with and we must test our assumptions fully and carefully before jumping to conclusions about how much tension is introduced into any given situation. This said, I am sure there are many senior leaders who thrive on high levels of tension and it is often our job as coaches to provide this, since others around them may not have the skills or the motivation to do so.

Systems thinking: In a way, John and Ian save the best until last with their model, since I believe that systems thinking is the underlying catalyst within their overall FACTS approach. Unfortunately, there is a severe shortage of people in the corporate world who look at the world through a systems thinking "lens." This leads to a focus on short-term, silo thinking, with a blindness to the wider context in which individuals are operating. While this mindset was not critical when the economic environment was stable and growing, it has suddenly become critical in a landscape where there is inherent instability, ambiguity, and contradiction. Systems thinking is not something any of us were taught at school, or indeed at business school, yet it is a discipline that will need to emerge from within each one of us as we face the unknowns of an increasingly interrelated world.

Models like GROW and FACTS are useful memory joggers or chronological sequences that coaches and others use or have handy; although models are just models, they are not the truth. There is no one way to coach any more than there is one way to walk. Each of us walks differently because our bodies are different. Each of us thinks differently because our brains are different. Were you taught to walk or did you just do it naturally over time? Being coached implies natural learning. It is only fair to say that the best coaching sessions you may have are often those that are intuitive and break all the rules. Each person needs to find their own natural and authentic way to coach that gets results over time, and we should never judge anyone else for not doing it our way.

In the later chapters of this book, John and Ian cast their net wider to consider the relevance of FACTS coaching to leaders and leadership. I have always held the view that "coaching is much bigger than coaching." There are trends ongoing in the world that will require new skills of our leaders. Old-style, autocratic leaders are losing their clout because the people they lead are becoming more challenging. As someone commented to me recently, "I used to interview people to work in this company, but now it feels like they interview me." In this environment, coaching skills become critical. How can you call yourself a leader in this new world if you do not have coaching skills? How can you lead by example? In Jim Collins' seminal book *Good to Great*, he suggests that a quality of "Level 5" leadership is humility. This is a word that is often misunderstood. It does not mean being a wimp: real humility is ruthlessly strong because it has a genuine authority at its core. John and Ian show how the FACTS model can help leaders deploy tough coaching skills with the humility that will be necessary to engage and motivate the modern workforce.

Challenging Coaching is an excellent contribution to the advancement of the profession of executive coaching. There are many books on the techniques of coaching, but what strikes me as unique about this book is that it focuses on the context in which coaching is taking place. John and Ian are taking the context of coaching seriously, and I hope that others will wake up to this important challenge through reading and re-reading this timely book.

Sir John Whitmore PhD, author of Coaching for Performance
December 2011

Warning: This is a provocative message!

When we have presented the themes in this book to our peers in the coaching world via many seminars, articles, and conferences over the past two years, our message has stirred up the profession in ways that we have found both surprising and unsettling. Our message has always provoked a strong reaction. In public, there are many who have suggested that the coaching approach we are proposing verges on the heretical. Indeed, one conference delegate suggested that our FACTS coaching model was akin to proposing that "the Pope was a Methodist." At another keynote speaker panel discussion, a stormy debate ended with a renowned coach launching into an expletive-ridden declaration: "Who do we think we are? We are not here to save the banking system. We're not here to save the planet. We forget we're a servant."

It has been an intense time. However, in private we have had many people approach us with words of great encouragement. Experienced, worldly coaches have whispered to us quietly: "I am so glad you are bringing these topics into the open." "It's about time someone raised these questions." "Keep up the good work." "This might not be a popular message, but it's an important one." "I'm a great fan of your approach."

We have been grateful for these sincere words against a backdrop of controversy, since they renewed our motivation and focus as we researched and wrote this book. At times when we have felt isolated among our own peers, we have consoled ourselves with the words of George Bernard Shaw: "All great truths begin as blasphemies." For sure, there are a number of coaching blasphemies in this book and it is unlikely you will read it without being provoked into adopting a strong opinion on its contents—either for or against!

With this in mind, read on...

CHAPTER 1
Time to face the FACTS of coaching

*What is overextended becomes diminished, what is too high
is cut down. (Tao Te Ching, Verse 36)*

One of the reasons we wrote this book is that we like a challenge. First, we want to stir up the young coaching profession by suggesting that it could be more than it currently is. Second, we want to help coaches learn new skills that can courageously challenge those they coach and so transform their potential and performance. In this sense, the coaching challenge starts with shining the spotlight on ourselves and then extends to explore the impact on those we work with and the results they deliver.

As experienced executive coaches we have worked with board-level executives around the globe and we've been struck by how these leaders thrive on challenge. And when we asked leaders for feedback on how our coaching could be made more impactful, repeatedly they replied: "I love it when you challenge me, so challenge me more!" These confident, ambitious individuals are surrounded by people who don't challenge them and, over time, this leads to an impoverished view of the world, impairs their decision making, and undermines business performance.

Yet, much of our own coach training was biased toward supporting others rather than challenging them. We noticed that this bias was also reflected in the many coaching books that exist and in the accrediting standards used by the different professional coaching bodies: an empathetic emphasis on listening and asking questions in a nondirective style, as opposed to a provocative emphasis on providing feedback and holding to account in an honest, direct style.

1

Prior to being executive coaches, we were senior business leaders in large, multinational organizations. We worked with board-level leaders who were surrounded by people who saw it as their job to agree with them, anticipate their needs, and accommodate their prejudices. For these leaders this created an illusion of reality that felt cosy and comfortable. Unless they were challenged honestly and openly, we noticed that these cosy clubs contained the seeds of their own destruction. Specifically, when the truth was not spoken for fear of upsetting others and the facts were not faced for fear of creating bad news, then a state of denial crept into the leadership psyche, robbing the organization of both its effectiveness and its moral compass.

In contrast, a healthy challenge, when delivered from a relationship of trust and mutual respect, serves to stretch people's thinking and drives them to dig deeper into the reality of their situation and the true potential of the future. And what is true for the chief executives and managing directors we coach is also true for every executive, regardless of seniority. In this climate, we have noticed our coachees showing new levels of creativity, motivation, and self-belief, leaving the coaching session inspired to prove to the world that they can be and will be more than they currently are. Maybe we are all stronger than others think we are? Maybe we all like a challenge when delivered by the right person in the right way?

This book is a rallying call to coaches and to everyone who is responsible for developing other people. Be the missing voice of challenge in the coaching conversation. Swallow hard and break the collective trance of the cosy club to reconnect senior leaders with reality through specific, direct, and concrete interventions. Get up close with the organization's future leaders to inspire them to pursue courageous goals—not in the service of individual egos, but toward a broader, collective purpose.

Creating the coaching mold

What we propose in this book is a coaching approach that breaks the mold. First, we need to understand how this mold came about and what factors influenced its design. Not many years ago few people in business had heard of the word coaching, but today it is a mainstream leadership skill and an established profession. The speed and extent with which coaching skills have been adopted in business life have been dramatic, resulting in a plethora of coaching businesses around the world and the routine training of line managers in coaching skills.

Why did this explosion in coaching occur? One of the most significant driving factors in business has been the emergence of the "war for talent." In a knowledge-based economy, attracting, developing, and retaining top talent are key determinants of organizational success. In the boom years, with talent in short supply, organizations seized on the idea of executive coaching as a way of recognizing and developing high-potential leaders. What had originally been regarded as a remedial activity quickly became a fashionable tool for the motivation and engagement of high performers. The argument was that if every top sports performer had a coach, why should the world of business be any different? Against this backdrop, there was a rapid growth in the use of executive coaching for senior leaders.

In parallel, the idea of a coaching culture emerged as an antidote to command and control. A younger, better-educated, and tech-savvy generation rebelled against authoritarian management styles and demanded greater empowerment. Many managers were trained in coaching skills as a response to this need. Armed with this new technique, they sought to build stronger relationships with managers that engaged and motivated rather than cajoled and bullied.

Hence, what shaped business coaching as it developed was a focus on individual wants, not organizational needs. Many return on investment (ROI) measures from coaching initiatives in this period reflected this bias, targeting the retention of high performers, improvement in staff survey engagement scores, and subjective feedback from participants rather than progress in specific, bottom-line measures.

Let us give you a typical example from this era. We designed and implemented a coaching program for a global property management company that was part of a Europe-wide leadership development program. The declared objectives of this program were as follows:

❑ Bring more rigor and objectivity to the succession planning process for the European board.
❑ Facilitate a greater number of cross-country and cross-business appointments in key roles.
❑ Motivate and retain key individuals by defining a clearer path to future career opportunities.
❑ Promote and embed the critical leadership competencies to deliver the three-year business vision.

Only the last of these objectives hinted at business performance measures; in practice, even the activity of developing leadership competencies was focused primarily on the development of personal skills rather than the delivery of collective business outcomes.

Participants in this program were allocated an external coach and an internal mentor for a series of individual coaching sessions focusing on the review of 360° feedback, the development of a career vision, and the practising of new skills. The participants in the program loved it. Engagement levels shot up, attrition levels shot down, new appointments were secured, and succession plans were put in place. When the program was formally evaluated, these were the headline benefits that were presented to the European board:

- ❑ Participants feel more motivated.
- ❑ Participants feel more valued.
- ❑ Participants have developed new insights into leadership behavior.
- ❑ Participants understand their career path better.
- ❑ Participants have expanded their networks.

From our perspective at that time, we were delighted with these outcomes. We did not realize then that we were focusing on a very narrow range of measures in an exceptionally strong business climate that had been booming for many years. These were "me, me, me" programs for a "me, me, me" business culture. As long as the good times rolled, everyone was happy. HR directors were doing what they wanted to do, coaches were doing what they wanted, CEOs were keeping their top people happy, and the formula worked well.

And then the world changed and the party was over. After 15 years of consecutive growth in the world's developed economies the "credit crunch" struck, heralding a wholesale recession. A temporary truce was established in the talent war as many thousands of companies froze recruitment and cut jobs. The property management company for which we'd developed a program suspended all training for two years, stopped bonuses, and introduced across-the-board pay cuts. This progressive modern company took these steps not because it suddenly didn't care about employee engagement and motivation, but because such measures were necessary to ensure business survival.

If you don't first secure the viability of the overall organization, what is the point of a succession plan or a motivated individual or high levels of employee engagement? For many in our generation of business leaders, this jolt represented a serious wake-up call.

Breaking the mold

We first noticed this shift while working with the sales management team of a well-known media company. This company had previously engaged a consultancy to train its area sales managers in coaching skills. All the managers attended a three-day coach skills training course and received follow-up support to apply their new skills. The courses focused on developing self-awareness through listening and asking open questions, as well as using the well-known GROW model.

The company experienced a dramatic fall in attrition levels among front-line salespeople due to improved relationships between the sales managers and those they managed. The new coaching skills helped motivate and engage staff and the program was considered a great success. However, the company then hit the early edge of the coming recession and launched an initiative to drive bottom-line performance in a more difficult marketplace. The area sales managers expressed concern that though their coaching skills had proved effective at building relationships, they were struggling to convert these relationships into bottom-line results in a tougher market environment. In response to this, some were clinging faithfully to their existing coaching style and others were reverting to a command-and-control approach. Neither response felt appropriate to the national sales director responsible for the team.

It was at this stage that we were commissioned to work with the sales managers as executive coaches. Given the history and the business need, we realized we would need to break the mold of the coaching style that had built up in this organization. We contracted with the group that we would introduce a new style of coaching that would build on and expand their existing skills. We advised them that they were going to learn "edgier" and more challenging behaviors that would introduce a level of tension into relationships with their teams. We asked them to trust that their relationships with the sales staff were now strong enough to withstand this tension and that the impact of a greater level of challenge in their coaching would be the improved bottom-line performance that was critical to collective success.

It was in this program that we first focused with a new level of intensity on the challenging coaching skills that form the basis of the approach in this book. While these skills had always been part of our repertoire, we "turned up the volume" on these behaviors—and we noticed a dramatic positive impact on the performance of our coachees and their teams. We started to break the mold of our own coaching styles in response to a changing business environment and gathered client feedback on the impact of these behaviors.

With these challenging skills came a changed ROI perspective for coaching. Whereas in the boom years coaching had been driven by a desire for a greater people focus, the same skills could generate wider performance outcomes by adjusting the balance between support and challenge in the coaching relationship. In parallel with a greater degree of challenge, the needs of other stakeholders in the organization were given equal and, in some cases, greater emphasis than the needs of the individual coachee. More rigorous contracting with these stakeholders throughout the coaching assignment brought a discipline and a reality check to the work by rooting coaching in organizational reality rather than leaving it to the whim of a single individual.

Initially, we thought that this approach was a unique response to one company's specific needs. However, in the years following we realized it was a more widespread response to the economic downturn, as more and more of our clients encouraged us to challenge them more strongly to achieve courageous goals and resolve tough issues. We concluded that the coaching mold must well and truly be broken and reformed if coaching is to mature and adapt to the new circumstances of twenty-first-century business.

Facing the FACTS

It was out of these experiences and front-line observations that the thinking and the models in this book were created. We distilled the essence of our experience into the five cornerstones of a more challenging coaching stance:

❑ **Feedback**—How does a coach provide challenging feedback that informs and inspires? How can we ensure that praise and recognition for a job well done are balanced with honest feedback on mistakes, learning, and failures? How can team collusion and compromise be avoided by skillful yet direct interventions?

❑ **Accountability**—How does a coach hold people accountable for commitments without blame or shame? How can accountability be extended from personal commitments to alignment with the values, strategy, and ethos of the wider organization? How can coaches anticipate the rising tide of accountability in the world at large and role model this behavior in their daily work?

❑ **Courageous goals**—How does a coach move beyond rational, incremental goal-setting models such as SMART to goal-setting models that engage the right-brain attributes of courage, excitement, inspiration, and transformation? What models and concepts help structure these conversations and provide a practical road map? What blocks this approach in the world of business?

❑ **Tension**—When is tension constructive? How can coaches practice creating and holding tension without risking burnout in key performers? How can the tension in a conversation be calibrated and dynamically adjusted to ensure peak performance? When does tension go too far and damage the underlying relationships?

❑ **Systems thinking**—How can a coach stay sensitive to "big-picture" issues such as ethics, diversity, and the environment without losing focus on bottom-line results? What can be learned from the world of systems thinking that enables the coach to be a positive agent of change for the wider organization? What is the role of intuition in guiding interventions that reach beyond the immediate coachee and touch on deeper organizational change?

By using the acronym FACTS we grounded the approach in a word that sums up a combination of realism, honesty, and challenge. FACTS is not to be regarded as a sequential series of steps like other models such as GROW, but as an integrated suite of thinking with dynamic elements that interact and overlap. The behaviors and skills in FACTS are not used *instead of* the supportive skills and models of more traditional coaching approaches, but rather to *expand* on these skills and leverage them to further improve performance and sustain the coaching impact. FACTS should be regarded as a development of coaching skills once the core skills have been mastered and a firm foundation of trust and respect has been established. From this starting point, a FACTS approach will provoke performance and change.

Who is this book for?

This book is intended for experienced coaches, business leaders who are keen to adopt a coaching style, and HR professionals who are promoting a coaching culture in their organizations. For coaches themselves, we hope that the book is a wake-up call regarding the need to adopt a more challenging style of coaching as opposed to the person-centered, supportive mindset in which the profession has been steeped to date. For business leaders, the book will provide practical tools and techniques that can be deployed in fifteen-minute business discussions as readily as they can in a two-hour coaching session. For HR professionals and other buyers of coaching, the book will provide a benchmark from which to assess coaching needs and a new language with which to assess coaches and their services. While we will refer to the "coach" throughout the book as our focus of attention, the reader should interpret this as applying not just to full-time, professional coaches, but to all those whose role and responsibility include the development of others to achieve a specific business outcome.

The messages in this book will be particularly relevant to any coach, line manager, or HR professional who is interested in answering the following questions:

❑ How should coaching skills evolve to suit a more challenging economic environment?

❑ How can coaching deliver outstanding bottom-line business results as well as build great personal relationships?

❑ How and when should a coach risk breaking rapport with a coachee in order to drive for a specific business result?

❑ How can coaching help move forward the wider leadership consciousness in business without compromising on its traditional ethics and values?

❑ What are the limits of the nondirective, person-centered coaching approach?

❑ Where does coaching go beyond the GROW model?

Challenging Coaching assumes that the reader has some knowledge and experience of basic coaching skills and models. For example, readers are likely to be familiar with common coaching models such as GROW and may have attended "Introduction to Coaching" courses where there is an emphasis on the skills of active listening and powerful questions applied in a nondirective coaching conversation. The book also assumes that the reader is familiar with the world of business, either from first-hand experience in a senior leadership role or through coaching leaders operating at this level in large, multinational organizations.

In a nutshell

The book is organized into three broad sections. First, Chapters 2 and 3 explore the theoretical background to our approach in detail. In Chapter 2 we introduce the support/challenge matrix, an empirical validation of our own coaching experience. The support/challenge matrix is a central premise of FACTS and is used throughout the book as a uniting theme. We will outline the concept of the ZOUD or Zone of Uncomfortable Debate, a concept that explores how to get to the "heart of the matter" in a coaching conversation by breaking rapport with the coachee and holding the tension of a difficult conversation. All of the skills in FACTS involve being able to enter and sustain the ZOUD in order to provoke performance and trigger change.

In Chapter 3 we explore the history of coaching in the business world in order to understand how the bias toward a supportive, person-centered mindset originated. In particular, we will look at how the world of therapy has influenced coaching and the advantages and disadvantages of this legacy. Finally, we will describe the core principles of FACTS and explore how these differ from the principles of traditional person-centered coaching. As part of this, various "sacred cows" of the coaching world will be put under the spotlight and challenged, including the non-directive principle, holding to the client's agenda, and the role of rapport.

In the second section of the book, Chapters 4 to 8, the practical skills in our coaching model are introduced and put to the test. Our intention is to provide simple, "real-world" tools and techniques that help the reader develop and practice new skills in a dynamic business context. Example dialogues, case studies, exercises, models, and metaphors are used to cater for different learning styles and provide fresh inspiration. The case studies we feature are not imaginary role plays but accurate accounts of real coaching sessions we have conducted. Where appropriate, we reference psychological models and business best practice to expand on themes and provide a strong empirical context. Throughout, our focus remains on the application of these skills in a business environment where multiple stakeholders, dynamic organizational structures, and shifting goals are the norm. We also assume a coachee who is routinely confident, ambitious, and resourceful in the pursuit of their goals—someone who has already mastered the basics of leadership and business, but who wishes to stretch to the next level in their development.

In the final section, Chapters 9 to 10, we look at the broader application of FACTS both now and into the future. Chapter 9 focuses on the specific role of a leader as coach to their own team and how FACTS can be applied on a day-to-day basis as part of a busy and demanding schedule. We introduce the idea of the player-coach, a leader who combines both "doing" and "coaching" to maximize the performance of others while still carrying out their own technical tasks and responsibilities. We explore this in practice by reviewing example FACTS dialogues for everyday management challenges such as delegation, managing performance, objective setting, managing upward, and client interaction.

Finally, Chapter 10 takes a philosophical turn to look at the wider implications of our coaching approach for the evolution of leadership in the twenty-first century. This is an ambitious chapter that shifts the agenda from discussing issues of support and challenge to the related and emotive issues of freedom and responsibility. It charts the evolution of dependent, independent, and interdependent mindsets and how a successful transition through each of these is facilitated by traditional coaching approaches and by FACTS.

This book is intended to challenge your view of coaching, to provoke you to think more deeply, and to help you learn valuable tools and techniques. Together we will step up to the coaching challenge—it is time to face the FACTS!

CHAPTER 2
From support to challenge

*It is easy to hold what is still stable, it is easy to mold what
is not yet formed. (Tao Te Ching, Verse 64)*

C oaching can help people move outside their comfort zone to
realize their latent potential and provoke long-term organizational change. But to do this, coaching must be more challenging
and move away from the notion that supporting the individual
alone is the most important factor for success.

In this chapter we examine in more detail this central premise of the FACTS model, having first assessed the risks associated
with traditional coaching. We introduce the support/challenge
matrix as a model for finding the right balance in a coaching relationship, and discuss the concept of the Zone of Uncomfortable
Debate (ZOUD).

The risks of traditional coaching

Traditional coaching comes from a supportive stance: helping an
individual develop. Most coaching literature and coach training
programs focus on the support skills needed to build trust and
rapport between coach and coachee. Showing genuine concern
for the client, attending to the client's agenda, summarizing,
paraphrasing, and mirroring back to ensure clarity, and asking
questions that reflect active listening—these are skills familiar
to all coaches and considered paramount for effective coaching.
Suggesting that we break away from these traditional skills seems
like sacrilege and so this supportive stance is not questioned.

However, the traditional approach carries the threefold risk of collusion, irrelevance, and self-obsession.

Collusion arises when the coach is only asking questions in a very supportive fashion, being nonjudgmental, and listening. Here, there is a risk that the coach colludes with the coachee; that is, aligns 100 percent with their worldview and fails to challenge or give feedback from a different perspective.

Irrelevance occurs when the coach always holds to the coachee's agenda regardless of the wider organizational context. In this situation, by the end of the second coaching session the coach might be helping to improve the coachee's golf swing rather than anything that aligns with bottom-line business performance. While this is a deliberately extreme example, how many coaches have asked themselves in the midst of a coaching session: "How did we get here and what on earth has this got to do with the people who are paying me to be in front of this person right now?"

Self-obsession is the risk of fueling the "me, me, me" attitude that many commentators believe had a significant impact on the lead-up to the financial crisis. Self-centered financial traders, focused solely on their own rewards, took risks that in hindsight had consequences for the wider organization and indeed the entire global banking system. Coaching concentrating purely on the coachee's agenda exacerbated this myopia, rather than developing a greater awareness of the wider context in which each person and each organization operated.

The risks of traditional coaching are more prevalent than the profession likes to recognize. They have crept up on us as the profession has grown and have not always been examined fully. In a sense, coaches accept these risks as "the devil they know," yet we could challenge ourselves harder to question the limitations of the traditional approach.

The support/challenge matrix

As we applied a more challenging stance in our own coaching work, we looked for a theoretical validation of our practical experiences. During this research we came across the simple graph below, which was first featured by Nevitt Sanford based on his research into the most appropriate learning environment for students; it was further developed by Daloz. The model suggests that optimum performance occurs when there is an effective balance between the levels of support and challenge provided by the coach. As a simple metaphor, consider an acorn that has the potential of becoming a great oak tree. In its growth the roots support it and the sun challenges it. It needs both "push" and "pull" if it is to reach its full potential.

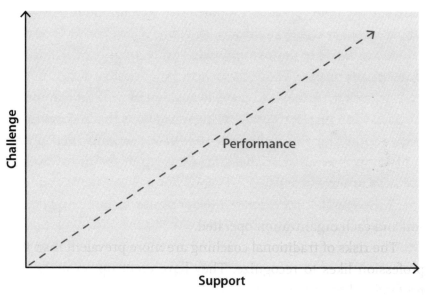

The diagram demonstrates that there are two variables at play here: support and challenge. It is when these two are out of balance that performance suffers. *Support* refers to interventions that affirm the value of the individual (building trust, respect, rapport)

or those that reduce uncertainty and anxiety (encouragement, focusing on strengths, empathy). *Challenge* refers to interventions that compel the individual to confront current reality (account-ability, feedback, limiting beliefs) and to meet the changing expec-tations of all stakeholders (goal setting, visioning, alignment of values).

Too often in business (and in life in general), people actively avoid challenging interventions, fearing that they will cause dis-ruption and create ill-will. However, a high level of challenge is not inherently "wrong." In fact, its absence in a business environ-ment leads to complacency, indulgence, apathy, and disinterest. When the stakes are high, a lack of challenge causes people to "play small" in an environment that is forever demanding that they "step up." The key is for challenge to be provided along-side equally high levels of support. The support skills of coach-ing are used to create conditions in which a coachee feels secure enough to disclose private thoughts and feelings, and in turn to develop awareness. There must also be challenge to push this self-awareness further and move to sustainable self-development. Coaches have invested considerable time and effort in developing their supporting skills; the next step in the development of the profession is to bring challenging skills up to the same level of maturity and proficiency.

We propose a conscious, intelligent use of both supporting and challenging skills where the coach can shift dynamically depending on the circumstances and the environment. The matrix opposite takes this support and challenge correlation further.

In the *low challenge/low support* quadrant, there is inertia and apathy. This environment is too dull, we become bored and disin-terested, and the "why bother?" question looms large, resulting in a lack of motivation to act. The *high challenge/low support* quadrant produces stress. This is a scary place in which we get frightened,

From support to challenge

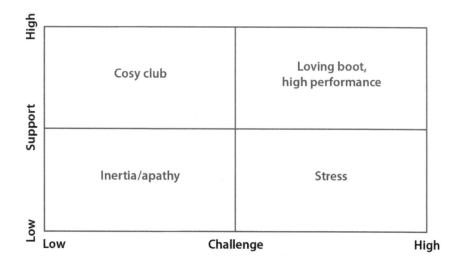

defensive, and hostile. The *low challenge/high support* quadrant is the "cosy club," which is too comfortable. In this zone there is high empathy, active listening, and questioning, but also the risks we discussed earlier, including collusion. The *high challenge/high support* area is where growth and development can be maximized. This is the "loving boot" that can stimulate and "kick" a person to pursue a new direction or goal and to achieve high performance. This quadrant represents the optimum balance of support and challenge where coaches can unlock the highest potential for both individual and organization.

When we talk to coaches about challenge, many say that they are already doing it, and then go on to talk about powerful questions to make the coachee stop and think, or the use of silence that may be uncomfortable but encourages depth of thought. There is nothing new here. We are talking about a greater degree of provocative challenge that pushes the coachee out of their comfort zone and forces them to confront issues, take risks, and drive headlong to achieve courageous goals.

The point of this 2x2 matrix is to encourage coaches to think about where they might be as the coaching sessions develop and as external circumstances change. This is an advanced coaching ability that does not happen without practice, diligence, and care. A train on a track can only go backwards and forwards and on a limited gradient. Compare this with an all-terrain vehicle, which has the power and ability to go in any direction as the environment changes. In coaching we have a preferred style and a default position. Link this with coach training that has focused only on a supportive approach, and without knowing it the coach is like the train, only able to go one way. However, if the coach develops awareness of the value of challenge, they will be more like the all-terrain vehicle, able to serve both individuals and the sponsoring organization more effectively and create sustained business change. This is about the coach's ability and choice—one default style is limiting, whereas a choice of approaches is robust and effective.

EXERCISE: SUPPORT/CHALLENGE

❑ Think about people you have coached and consider the diagram below, which represents a support–challenge continuum.

Support	*Challenge*
• Shows genuine concern	Positively confronts •
• Demonstrates respect	Holds the client accountable •
• Attends to client's agenda	Challenges assumptions •
• Summarizes, paraphrases...	Provides feedback •
• Active listening	Uses intuition •
• Acknowledges the client	Takes risks (feels unsafe) •
• Feels comforted	

```
 ├──┼──┼──┼──┼──┼──┼──┼──┼──┼──┤
 0   1   2   3   4   5   6   7   8   9   10
```

Produces strong rapport and relationship   **Produces strong business results**

❑ Where is your natural starting point? If you are naturally support-ive you may assess yourself at 1; however, if you are more challeng-ing you may assess yourself at 8, for example. Give yourself a score as a starting point.

❑ If you were to ask the people you have coached, what would they say? Would it be different to or the same as your own assessment?

❑ Now consider the most outrageous, ridiculous, and challenging things you could do or say. Be free, do not edit your thoughts, and do not think of the consequences at this stage.

❑ What would it take for you to do or say some of these things?

❑ How would these be received by the people you coach?

❑ Based on any difference between your self-assessment and the assessment other people might give you, can you risk being more challenging?

The zone of uncomfortable debate

The view that coaching conversations can be both supportive and challenging is reinforced by a model developed by Professor Cliff Bowman from Cranfield University, UK. In the diagram overleaf, the center represents the core of the issue, which, once discussed, provides the key to making a breakthrough: moving understand-ing to the next level, or moving an idea forward, or unblocking a problem, or resolving an argument. Around this are two concen-tric layers: the outer layer is the "zone of comfortable debate" and the inner layer is the "zone of uncomfortable debate" (ZOUD).

When an interaction begins between two or more people, there is typically a period of small talk and developing an under-standing of common ground. This is where the conversation is nice, it's easy, it feels relaxed, and there's not a lot of tension. The people are chatting about simple, obvious things, for example

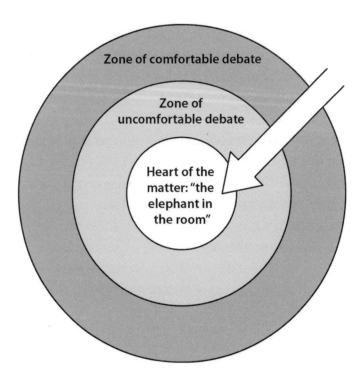

catching up on news and gossip, what has happened since they last met, common interests such as sport and family, and exchanging basic information. This stage of the conversation is in the zone of comfortable debate and is straightforward.

If this conversation is to be more than a social chat, there is usually something important to discuss. The parties have come together for a purpose: to agree action, to make a decision, to resolve a problem. To achieve this end, a social, comfortable conversation is not sufficient—to get to the heart of the issue the conversation must move to a ZOUD. In this zone there is a feeling of increased tension and the pressure starts to build as the parties may disagree and may not see "eye to eye." What often happens is that the individuals feel the tension, find it uncomfortable, and, fearing that the pressure will permanently damage the relationship, move back out to the zone of comfortable debate.

The tension is diffused and the rapport is maintained, but the matter at hand has not been resolved. The core issue is still the same and no progress has been made. The conversation must stay in the ZOUD and the parties work through it to uncover differences in understanding, assumptions, motives, and so on. By sustaining the ZOUD they can resolve the issue permanently and move on to a new topic.

This is a bit like having an "elephant in the room," something enormous that is taking up significant space. The elephant is such a big and difficult animal that it is not dealt with directly. Perhaps people don't want to make the elephant angry in case it damages the whole house, or maybe they are too polite to comment on it. What happens is that they find innovative and creative ways to move around the elephant and manage it and live with it. Until they face up to the fact that there is actually an elephant in the room and try to remove it directly, the situation will remain unchanged.

So what is the connection between this model of communication and coaching? Coaches often work in difficult areas of personal development. If these areas were simple to understand and easy to resolve, the individual would not need a coach, they would simply sort it out themselves. Often coaching is about holding up a mirror and showing the coachee something they do not want to see and have avoided up to now. Effective coaching is about challenging assumptions, examining habits, overcoming barriers, and embedding change. For this to work, the coach must give feedback, challenge the coachee to be accountable, and be prepared to go into the ZOUD to hold the tension until the "heart of the matter" is opened up and resolved. All the components of challenging coaching require the coach to enter the ZOUD more often, more skillfully, and with total belief that this is being done in the best long-term interests of the coaching relationship.

In the ZOUD there is a risk that the coachee may lose resourcefulness, may feel tense and stressed, and may lack the ability to draw on their natural abilities. This loss of resourcefulness signals that it is time to revert to supportive coaching skills so that a balance is struck and resourcefulness restored. At this point the coach does not exit the ZOUD, but offers a supporting statement, or an observation about how the coachee is feeling, which enables them to take a breath, regroup, and then move forward again through the ZOUD.

It is important to recognize that the coach can experience the same feelings and thoughts as the coachee while in the ZOUD. The coach can lose resourcefulness and may be outside their comfort zone, leading to the natural inclination to reduce the challenge and move back to the zone of comfortable debate. Again, an authentic statement such as "I can feel real tension here" helps connect the coach and the coachee, as they both know what the other feels and this breaks the tension for a moment before moving on.

Have you ever done something so difficult that you felt like giving up? For example, this could have been running a marathon for the first time. Runners describe "hitting the wall" and, in a physical sense, this is like encountering the ZOUD. With determination, visualization of the finish line, and maybe a pause for breath, the runner regains the physical and mental resources to continue the marathon. So when a coachee or a coach "hits the wall," take a breath, recover, and then continue.

Some coaches have difficulty with this concept. Many believe that they are there to serve and support the coachee. Wanting to be the peacemaker, a coach may feel the need to maintain harmony and find "common ground," and so diffuse the tension by going back into the zone of comfortable debate and creating innovative strategies to approach the subject in a different way that is less tense. The challenge for the coach is to stay in the ZOUD and hold direct as opposed to directive communication.

So what will enable a coach to enter and work with the ZOUD? This is about the coach's belief. High-potential individuals are typically robust and able to participate in strong debate. The coach is there to serve the coachee and the organization sponsoring the coaching, so any intervention will be designed to be positive and constructive. The coach feels the challenge of the ZOUD and has the confident belief that this will lead to a breakthrough. The tension can be diffused by the coachee, who taps into this energy and makes the shift. If the coaching relationship is built on solid support skills, it will be strong enough to sustain that amount of challenge and benefit from facing rather than avoiding the heart of the issue.

The concept of the ZOUD is fundamental to all components of the FACTS coaching approach. Every element of FACTS (Feedback, Accountability, Courageous goals, Tension, and Systems thinking) requires the coach to have an awareness of the ZOUD and the ability to enter into it consciously when the situation demands. With this approach we are challenging both the coach and the coachee to be greater than they currently are, to push further, and to expect more from themselves.

Working in all four quadrants

In this chapter we have explored the risks of traditional coaching. When coaching is oriented to supporting the individual coachee, the risks of collusion, irrelevance, and self-obsession result in a coaching relationship that, over time, does not deliver the fullest potential for either the coachee or the sponsoring organization. Our own experience working with senior leaders is that a more challenging coaching stance can drive performance to a deeper and more sustained level.

The four quadrants of the support/challenge matrix reveal the goal of high support/high challenge coaching, which avoids both the "cosy club" of high support/low challenge and the stress and relationship breakdown of high challenge/low support. Our vision is for the coach to work dynamically in all four quadrants of the matrix depending on the precise circumstances of the coachee and the organization.

Similarly, the ability to work confidently and skillfully in the zone of uncomfortable debate is key to shifting from the high support/low challenge quadrant to high support/high challenge. Coaches who can provoke their coachees to move out of their comfort zone will be experienced as a "loving boot"—they will administer a "kick" in performance and potential while remaining rooted in a pure intention to help. The support/challenge matrix and the concept of working in the ZOUD lie at the heart of all that will follow in subsequent chapters as we develop the detailed principles and skills of the FACTS approach.

EXERCISE: ZOUD

- ❏ Reflect on a time when you entered the ZOUD. What happened?
- ❏ When have you held the tension, and when have you diffused it? What does this tell you?
- ❏ What core assumptions do you hold about tension and the importance of rapport?
- ❏ What is the difference between direct and directive communication?
- ❏ What are the conditions that will enable you as a coach to enter the ZOUD and work within it?

CHAPTER 3
The core principles of FACTS

Truth can appear as lie, straightness can appear as twisted.
(Tao Te Ching, Verse 45)

In Chapter 2 we saw that coaching has the potential to have a greater impact on individuals and organizations through challenge. But something is holding back coaching and preventing it from embracing the change that is needed. Coaching is rooted in the past, with links to the sister professions that have strongly influenced its development.

In this chapter we explore this further and look at the evolution of coaching relative to other "support" professions such as therapy, mentoring, and consulting. We consider the validity of the underlying principles of traditional coaching and describe the new principles that support FACTS coaching. The changes we describe are fundamental for the long-term impact of coaching and for organizational effectiveness.

The evolution of coaching

In a Darwinian sense, the professions of medicine, engineering, and accountancy are the metaphorical equivalents of *homo sapiens*. They have existed for hundreds of years and have grown through every stage of the economic cycle, refining and adapting their practices, their standards, and their ethics. However, coaching is an emerging profession: Sir John Whitmore and Graham Alexander pioneered it in the 1980s and the International Coach Federation was established in 1995, the Association for Coaching in 2002.

Thus coaching is nothing more than a blip on the evolutionary scale compared to other professions. Is coaching the amoeba, the fish, or the amphibian of the professional world? And even in this short timespan, the coaching profession has changed, developed, and adapted. We have seen coaches specializing in specific tools and techniques, such as the GROW model, co-active coaching, NLP, Gestalt, and the solutions focus movement. Within 20 years, coaching has grown rapidly and become accepted as a mainstream leadership weapon in the war for talent.

However, evolution does not stop and the coaching profession must recognize changing performance challenges and adapt accordingly. Consider the evolution of the dinosaurs, masters of the planet for millions of years. Extinction followed huge environmental change caused by massive volcanic eruptions across the world. The dinosaurs could not cope with this catastrophic environmental event and death followed. Will coaching evolve with the current seismic shifts in the economic environment, or will the profession and its practice remain rooted in the past and risk extinction?

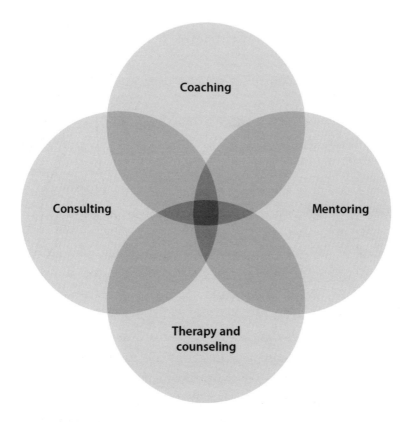

The diagram above shows the overlap with other disciplines designed to support and develop people and organizations. Have these influences on the young coaching profession had a positive or a negative impact?

There are common aspects that link all of these disciplines, skills and behaviors that support the individual in the broadest sense—active listening and powerful questioning. Distilled down, these two skill sets link coaching, therapy, consulting, and mentoring. These are the skills that are crucial for developing understanding and awareness, the starting point for any change process. Fundamentally, these are the skills required for effective communication; only the application will vary depending on the situation, whether it is supporting a patient through trauma or working with an executive to achieve more within their business.

Therapy and counseling have had a great impact on coaching. In particular, the work of Carl Rogers and Gerard Egan has had a direct impact on the ethical and philosophical underpinnings of the coaching mindset.

Person-centered therapy

Carl Rogers was one of the most influential thought leaders within the profession of counseling. In the 1940s and 1950s, he developed the person-centered therapeutic approach, which suggested that the therapist could be of most help to clients by allowing them to find their own solutions to their problems. This was a nondirective approach in which therapists hold the belief that clients have within themselves vast resources for development. Clients have the capacity to grow and the therapist's role is to create the conditions in which this growth is encouraged. The core conditions for this are empathy (the ability to sense the client's world as if it were your own, active listening, summarizing, reflecting, paraphrasing, clarifying, acknowledging), congruence (the therapist being open to their own feelings, without front or façade, saying what they think or feel), and unconditional positive regard (nonjudgmental acceptance, each person is worthy, hate the sin but love the sinner).

Gerard Egan built on Rogers' approach in his book *The Skilled Helper* in 1982, developing a three-stage model:

❏ *Stage 1*—Building a relationship and exploration: empathy, congruence, unconditional positive regard.
❏ *Stage 2*—New understanding, different perspectives: focus on issues, challenging perspectives, goal setting.

❏ *Stage 3*—Action: developing new strategies, action plans, evaluating consequences.

These approaches will feel incredibly familiar to coaches. Many coach training programs and coaching texts relate closely to the principles described by Rogers and Egan. Returning to our evolutionary metaphor, coaching and therapy share a significant proportion of their DNA and could be regarded as having emerged from the same "swamp." If we take two popular approaches to coaching we can further explore this shared DNA.

Consider the co-active coaching model, described by Laura Whitworth and colleagues in *Co-Active Coaching*, and its four cornerstones:

❏ The client is naturally creative, resourceful, and whole.
❏ Co-active coaching addresses the client's whole life.
❏ The agenda comes from the client.
❏ The relationship is a designed alliance.

There is significant overlap here with Carl Rogers' work. The resourceful and creative client links with his notion that the client has vast resources for development. Rogers' nondirective person-centered approach means that the agenda comes from the individual (not the therapist or any other person). The therapist's role is to create the conditions for growth, so the relationship is a designed alliance.

The popular GROW model, developed by Graham Alexander and Sir John Whitmore, describes the simple yet powerful process exploring goals, reality, options, and willingness to act. Just like Rogers, the GROW model assumes that the coachee is able to find their own solutions, with a focus on strong empathy, and it follows Egan's approach of developing understanding and moving to action.

The result of this influence is that the skills at the heart of coaching are largely oriented toward counseling skills with a nondirective ethos, majoring on listening skills and the ability to ask powerful questions, and so demonstrating empathy and building a strong rapport between coach and client. These traditional skills are replicated in the coaching competency frameworks set out by the various professional bodies.

The ground trodden by therapists has enabled the coaching profession to develop very rapidly. The core principles of therapy have been used to provide a structure, an ethical basis, and fundamental principles. If coaching had not evolved from therapy, it would have taken significantly longer to develop to the current state of professionalism, so this evolutionary route has served coaching well up to a point. However, it has also caused limitations. Has coaching sucked in too much from therapy, particularly as the business environment changed? Do person-centered therapeutic models really provide the level of challenge that will stretch executives to approach situations in new ways, break from old habits, and look at the long-term impact of personal decisions across the whole business?

The core principles of traditional coaching

The three principles of traditional coaching are like the sacred columns supporting the temple of person-centered coaching. These columns are:

❑ A nondirective approach
❑ Holding to the individual's agenda
❑ Building rapport

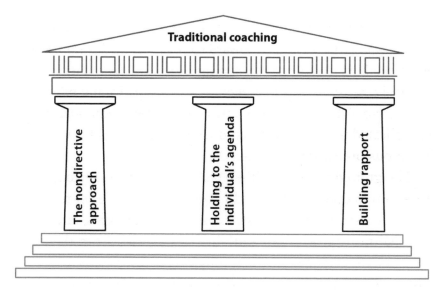

It is as if these columns are viewed with such reverence that they are not questioned or challenged. Coaching literature and training courses emphasize the importance of these principles. They are at the heart of the coaching philosophy of many coaches and professional bodies. We will look at each pillar in turn and question its relevance to our expanded vision for a challenging coaching role.

A nondirective approach

The nondirective principle requires that the coach does not direct the topic or discussion within the coaching session. It is the most deeply rooted principle in person-centered coaching and hence we will explore it in greater detail than the other two. In essence, it states that a coach must not direct the agenda and so it is not for the coach to say what areas the coachee should discuss. A nondirective approach assumes that the coachee is the best person to solve the issue and has the answers within them. It holds more developmental possibilities as it helps the coachee develop their own solutions. Take the example of co-active coaching, which assumes that the coachee is whole, resourceful, and naturally creative. If you accept this perspective, the coach is there simply to ask questions, listen, and empower the coachee to elicit the skills of creativity they already possess.

Nondirective coaches should not give advice, as this would influence the coachee's choices. The role is thus very different to that of a consultant or mentor. A nondirective coach should leave no trace of their presence. Coach training programs encourage the development of "plain vanilla" coaches who are required to be completely nondirective. However, once trainee coaches have passed their assessment and achieved accreditation, reality kicks in and each coach's personality comes into play based on their prior knowledge and experience.

Take the example of Steve, who had been a management consultant for 20 years and was studying with a reputable coaching school. The school was encouraging him to hold back all his prior knowledge and consulting experience and coach from a purely nondirective stance. Steve was finding this stifling and felt that it was not in the best service of his coachees, as he had a lot more to offer. In the nondirective world it is as if we are learning to drive on empty roads and there are no other cars, stationary or moving. This is clearly artificial and a newly qualified driver will not know how to negotiate moving vehicles, so a crash is almost inevitable. Should we not be training coaches to deal with real situations so that they are congruent and authentic rather than fixed to one contrived approach?

The reality of the situation is that nondirective coaching is a myth. Coaches are coaching experts and inevitably direct and steer the process toward achieving the desired results as identified by the coachee and sponsoring organization. Given the nuances of body language, tone of voice, expression, and so on, it is almost impossible for a coach to be nondirective. In fact, a coach should be free to ask more directive questions that push an issue, indicate another possible consideration (a hypothesis the coach has developed through listening actively), or insert an opportunity to look at something differently. Occasionally a coachee may not trust their own ability to think deeply or long enough to offer alternative options; they may have ideas but not the confidence to voice them. In such a situation, the fact that the coach is offering suggestions may create a breakthrough and provide confidence in the coachee that what they were thinking but not speaking was valid. This can provide positive reinforcement and ideas will be able to flow more freely from the coachee in the future.

There is a difference between offering advice and suggestions and directing the coachee to a solution predetermined by the coach. For example, if a coachee is stuck and has ground to a halt, as is often the case, a coach can kick-start their thinking by offering suggestions. Once the coachee has exhausted their options, the coach can offer advice: "Have you considered this option...?" Such suggestions and advice will spark off the client's ability to think more creatively and move forward.

We recall a session where one of the authors was coached and felt stuck, uncertain of the next step to take, and the coach asked: "Who have you spoken to about this?" This was clearly a directive question and was asked of a known introvert in Myers-Briggs Type Indicator terms (someone who would try to solve everything for themselves in their head). This started a new train of thought and unblocked the situation, and has been remembered ever since.

What is important is that the coachee takes an idea and runs with it, developing an approach for themselves after weighing up all the possibilities. If a coach is in the service of the coachee and the sponsoring organization, does it matter if an intervention is directive or nondirective? As coaches we should provide a service that gives the coachee and the organization what they want and need and use all our available coaching skills. The coach may have some experience, knowledge, or information that the coachee does not, and if the coach holds back for fear of being directive, surely this is disingenuous and not in the best service of the coachee? Does the coachee or sponsor care about being directive or nondirective as long as it produces sustainable results?

To be clear, we are not suggesting that executive coaches revert to the "tell and do" approach. We are not justifying lazy or poor practice in developing people. This is about skill and judgment, combined with the ability to use every form of intervention. The ability to be more direct also relates to the maturity of the relationship—a coaching comment or question can be more direct in a more mature relationship. If a coach is too direct too early, this can create dependency and/or push-back from the coachee. If the relationship is mature, self-sufficiency will have been created so that there is interdependence and not dependence. It is valid for a coach to advise and direct, but only with active listening, powerful questioning, and once the coachee has exhausted all other options.

This also highlights the difference between coaching and the other supporting processes of counseling, consulting, and mentoring. It is likely that consultants and mentors will advise and direct much more often than coaches and earlier in the relationship; after all, this is what clients are paying for and expecting. However, counselors may never move to advice or direction due to the person-centered nature of the therapeutic intervention.

Holding to the individual's agenda

We will now move to the second column in the temple of traditional coaching, holding to the individual's agenda. We believe that this principle is limiting. In Chapter 2 we talked about the risks of traditional coaching as collusion, irrelevance, and self-obsession. All of these risks come into play because of rigid adherence to the coachee's agenda. However, we all know that there are times when a coachee will avoid issues that are uncomfortable but essential to achieving the desired outcome. A coach must be able to challenge and highlight avoidance and direct the conversation to address these matters and get into the ZOUD.

In addition, many coaches face the situation where a coachee wants to tackle a seemingly ordinary topic, but through discussion and exploring this further the coach suspects that there is something deeper and that the key issue is different to that originally outlined by the coachee. In the moment the coach must be free to tell it as it is, to speak the unspoken and take the agenda into a new area. A coaching session may develop an insight into a coachee's blind spot, and shifting the agenda through feedback to direct questions will develop awareness and move the coachee forward.

The wider context here is that if the coach focuses only on the coachee's agenda, the needs of the sponsoring organization may be ignored. It is vital that coaching is linked to the achievement of wider business results. A focus on the coachee's agenda is too narrow. Through effective contracting at the beginning of the coaching assignment, the coach can involve the line manager, the human resource professional, and the coachee in establishing objectives that engage all stakeholders.

Building rapport

The final column in the traditional coaching temple is building rapport. This states that effective coaching is built on strong empathy between the coach and coachee, which leads to trust and rapport. In therapy, Carl Rogers believed that through respect and empathy the client will be at the center of the helping process and be best placed to feel safe to explore issues. This feeling of safety and security is fundamental in a therapeutic setting, working to help a sensitive and dysfunctional client. However, in coaching we work with robust and functioning people who can be pushed, challenged, and provoked. Therefore, regarding the act of building rapport as sacrosanct may limit coaching interventions.

The coach cannot enter the ZOUD if they will not risk breaking rapport. The greatness within a coachee cannot be freed if the coach holds a functioning coachee in a safe place, which in fact cocoons them unnecessarily. We are not talking about a pendulum swing from too much support to all challenge; empathy, trust, and rapport are key foundations for effective coaching and these must be in place. However, they are necessary but not sufficient: there must be more for coaching to be at its most effective.

The core principles of FACTS coaching

We have challenged some of the core principles of traditional coaching with the aim of stripping it of unhelpful dogma. However, it is one thing to criticize an existing construct, quite another to propose a creative alternative. We will now build the new columns that hold up the FACTS coaching model, the foundational values that capture the essence of this style of coaching. Three of these principles will be familiar to coaches—the "hidden

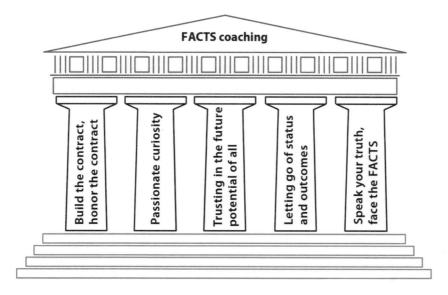

treasures"—and two are likely to be unfamiliar—what we call "new gems."

The columns on which the FACTS model rests are the hidden treasures:

❏ Passionate curiosity
❏ Trusting the future potential of all
❏ Letting go of status, expertise, and outcomes

And the new gems:

❏ Build the contract, honor the contract
❏ Speak your truth, face the FACTS

You may be familiar with the story of Angkor Wat, a vast temple in Cambodia. It was built in the twelfth century but was abandoned and left for the jungle to take over, remaining hidden for many years. Eventually, the jungle was cut back to reveal a unique hidden treasure that now attracts many thousands of visitors each year. Hidden treasures like this can be covered by "jungle," overlooked and forgotten, but once rediscovered they can provide great insight. The hidden treasures in coaching are principles that have always existed but are still worth highlighting.

Passionate curiosity

Passionate people care and curious people want to find out more and make a difference. A passionately curious person is not judgmental, but listens and clarifies. Carl Rogers would describe this as unconditional positive regard for the individual—a focus on "the act rather than the actor," "the sin rather than the sinner." Although we have criticized the wholesale sucking in of therapeutic principles, this unconditional positive regard is at the center of FACTS coaching; the difference here is that it is within the context of an organization, not the individual alone. A passionately curious coach will ask and listen to understand the immediate, short-, and long-term organizational context and will represent the interest of wider stakeholders, with the intention of enhancing the performance of the coachee and the business as a whole.

We are all curious to different degrees, interested in other people. However, few of us practice curiosity and develop this natural skill beyond a basic level. We don't tend to elevate curiosity from a skill to a passion and a value, but this is what is required of the coach. Curiosity is related to a nonjudgmental attitude, in that the curious coach observes with all their senses and focuses all their energy on understanding rather than evaluating and coming to conclusions. Often such conclusions serve to reinforce existing prejudices, as opposed to representing genuine attempts to understand the unique reality of the person or the moment.

A curious attitude is motivated not by the need to be right, but by the need to understand. In the words of Stephen Covey in *The Seven Habits of Highly Effective People*: "Seek first to understand and then to be understood." The passionately curious coach listens and observes, like a radio telescope collecting data on many wavelengths. They develop a focus of attention, sensitivity to feelings, and understanding of facts that is both profound and inspiring to those who are in their presence. It is the purity of this curiosity that is powerful and the primary evidence of its existence is the behavior of listening.

A by-product of such relentless curiosity is that, temporarily, the coach detaches from the outcome of the conversation. They appear no longer to care about how they are performing or whether they are achieving their own goals. This caring detachment creates a space in which everyone can feel free to express views, generate ideas, register dissent, and contribute their all to the cause. Collective awareness builds and the correct solution emerges naturally, rather than as a forced, prescriptive conclusion.

Trust in the future potential of all

In an organizational context, most employees are professional, qualified, and skillful, and want to make a positive contribution (the few exceptions to this rule we remember vividly, but they should not distort our view of the many). The individual is resourceful and able to grow and change in response to challenge. If we did not hold a belief in the coachee's greatness as a core principle, then why would we be in the business of developing people?

The role of a coach is to see potential where no one else sees it: to have more faith in the potential of others than they might have in themselves, to seek the little acorns and trust that they will grow into mighty oak trees. If someone came up to you in the office and said "I want to be CEO of this company in ten years' time," what would you do? Would you laugh, would you see arrogance, would you view it as a personal threat to your own ambitions? Adidas claims that "Nothing is impossible." Do you see this as clever marketing or as a truth? Do you believe in miracles? Or deep down do you think that people will always be what they have always been and should be managed accordingly?

In business it is not fashionable to believe in miracles. There are leaders who have reached the limit of their faith in people, whose trust has been betrayed many times, whose patience has been sorely tested, and who have experienced failure in themselves and others. How do you find faith again and again and rekindle trust in the potential of others again and again when the reality of daily business life is that things go wrong, goalposts move, and people let you down? Surely a logical response is to lower your expectations, temper your goals, and prepare for the worst?

There is no "magic wand." Trust in the future potential of all can only come about through the experience of "wiping the slate clean" each day and recommitting to the possibilities rather than the constraints of people and circumstances. However it is done, this principle is essential to the empowering presence of a challenging coach, as such a coach knows that within each person there is latent potential that needs to be released.

Letting go of status, expertise, and outcomes

The third column of hidden treasures ensures that the coach is in the service of the coachee and the sponsoring organization, not of their own ego. To serve in this way the coach must let go of power and status; these are no longer important and are not drivers, motivators, or something the coach strives for. In transactional analysis terms, the coach will comfortably and confidently maintain adult-to-adult interactions. "I am not the expert, and I don't need to be the expert" is a mantra that the most effective coaches will feel very comfortable saying. They do not need to know the answer, or to demonstrate their effectiveness through an impressive theatrical performance. By being detached from the outcome, the coach holds the coachee fully accountable for their own development and keeps ownership squarely resting on the coachee's shoulders. The phrase "detached from the outcome" does not imply a lack of care since, as we described above, passionate curiosity remains crucial.

It is easier to let go if you are an external coach than if you are an internal coach operating within the organizational system. When you are part of organizational politics and you have your own objectives to achieve, then detaching your ego from the situation is incredibly difficult. We all have instances where our buttons are pressed and our ability to stay detached is challenged. Over time and with improved self-awareness, it is as if our buttons become smaller and our reactions to them being pressed become more controllable. Our wisdom and confidence develop, allowing us to take more risks and to experiment with letting go.

Build the contract, honor the contract

This is the first of the "new gems" of FACTS coaching. A contract can be in the form of a deal, an agreement, a promise, between a leader and a follower, a coach and a coachee, a parent and a child, a husband and a wife, two friends, a seller and a purchaser. We implicitly make informal contracts and agree that one person will do something in return for someone else doing another thing.

Some of these agreements are small, and some are very large and life changing, such as entering into marriage. However, realistically we cannot uphold every agreement, because circumstances change. Priorities alter, people are late for meetings, marriages break up, every day there are conversations along the following lines: "Yes, I did agree to meet you at 6 pm, but I couldn't make it because I needed to go to the shops." Contracts are continually established, updated, and reviewed, and some come to an agreed or abrupt conclusion.

Some contracts are captured in formal, legal documentation; others are informal, relying to a greater degree on trust and the spoken word. Some contracts are explicit, others are implicit. Sometimes agreements and contracts are entered into too easily or flippantly in order to please other people, or to get other people "off your back," so there is no basis for honoring them as there was no real commitment in the first place.

When someone begins employment with a company, there is a legal set of terms and conditions that govern their relationship with the employer. The newly hired person commits to observe this agreement and performs a job in return for a wage, holidays, and other benefits. They also agree to submit to the consequences should they break their part of the deal through poor performance or misconduct. This level of contracting is familiar and something we honor as a natural course of our professional lives. This contract is signed and then consigned to a filing cabinet, and neither party expects to look at it again unless something serious and unexpected happens in the relationship.

A formal contract is one thing, but how do we manage the variety of informal contracts we enter into on a daily basis? How do we build them and how do we honor them? This type of contract is implicit and psychological rather than explicit and legal. A psychological contract develops in an ad hoc, "trial and error" fashion and covers informal, mutual obligations between two people. Nevertheless, problems can occur as people make assumptions and interpret things differently, so the contract may be unknowingly broken, resulting in a loss of trust and respect.

Take the unstated psychological contract between a sales manager and a newly recruited sales executive. Interviews have been held, psychometric tests completed, and contracts signed. In the first week of the new role, the sales executive is issued with a sales target for the following 12 months and a bonus scheme agreement. As she tries to find her way in the new company, the following happen:

- ❑ In month one, the sales executive upsets a client.
- ❑ In month three, she upsets a colleague.
- ❑ In month five, she sells a piece of work.
- ❑ In month seven, the sales executive leaves by mutual agreement. She is paid a "compromise agreement" sum in return for not pursuing a case of wrongful dismissal. She is offered a positive reference for a future employer and the recruitment process starts again.

Contrast this experience with the same sales executive who begins work with an organization populated by coaching leaders who pride themselves on building and honoring strong psychological contracts with their followers:

- ❑ In month one, the contract is built by explicitly stating what is expected in terms of standards of behavior (in the form of company values or a competency framework) and standards of performance in terms of agreed work objectives and reporting back. The sales executive and sales manager agree review meetings every two weeks.

❑ In month three, the sales executive has integrated into the culture of the business and is fully aware of what is expected; there is a good cultural and team fit. Some underachievement of objectives has been discussed openly with the sales manager, who accepts that the sales executive is new and cannot be expected to perform like an established member of the team. The manager coaches the sales executive in specific areas and further development goals have been agreed.

❑ In month five, performance is going well; the sales executive is motivated and happy that she has made the right move to the new company. Review meetings are now monthly; these are coaching sessions focused on performance and achievement of objectives, supported by open and timely communication between sessions.

❑ In month seven, the sales executive achieves the highest sales figures across the company coupled with consistently positive feedback from clients.

The difference in the second scenario is the depth of understanding and mutual commitment, developed though talking in an adult-to-adult way to build an explicit psychological contract. Assumptions are shared in an environment of trust and respect.

Moving to the arena of a coaching relationship, good practice suggests that there is a formal coaching agreement stating the number of sessions, duration, cancellation arrangements, ethical standards, confidentiality, boundaries, arrangements for ending the relationship, and evaluation. Even coaching relationships end prematurely or do not achieve the intended outcome. Nevertheless, much is left in the informal and unwritten zone of implied agreements. For coaching to be as effective as possible, the coach should be explicit at the beginning and throughout, and by questioning encourage the coachee to state any assumptions and open these up for discussion. The psychological contract between coach and coachee should be specifically reviewed on a periodic basis to ensure that both parties feel the agreement is being honored and have the opportunity to refine, adapt, or end the engagement.

Whenever a coach is seeking to build an explicit psychological contract, they will hear themselves using the following statements repeatedly:

❑ "What I expect from you is..."
❑ "What you can expect from me is..."
❑ "If either of us breaks the rules then these are the consequences..."
❑ "Is this OK?"
❑ "What help do you need from me to honor this?"
❑ "We need to review this agreement periodically and update it to reflect changing circumstances. Let's meet to do that in..."

Likewise, when reviewing the contract to ensure it is still being honored by both parties, coaches will overhear themselves using the following phrases:

❑ "So, what is your view on how things have been going since we last met?"
❑ "Here is my honest perspective of the situation..."
❑ "How is our original agreement standing up to the test of reality? What is working? What isn't working?"
❑ "How am I doing in helping you with all of this? Where can I improve?"
❑ "What, if anything, do we need to change in our agreement to reflect new circumstances and future goals?"
❑ "What are your limits in all of this? What are my limits?"

❑ "What creative perspectives have we missed that will release even greater potential in our relationship?"

Without a strong written and spoken psychological contract in place, there is no personal legitimacy in the coaching relationship. There is no basis on which to build and no boundary to maintain. There is nothing for either party to feel responsible for, hence no real definition of success or failure. The key is that these are personal conversations conducted in the first person, not organizational conversations conducted in the third person. This is *your* relationship: own it, put a human face on it, bring your whole self to it, and make it a shining example of your coaching presence.

There is another layer to this thinking. In religious settings the word "covenant" is often used, meaning a solemn promise. This puts a whole new depth on the idea of an agreement and a psychological contract between two parties. A solemn promise is serious stuff. So can we make our agreements like covenants, rather than the easily broken written or spoken contracts that pervade some areas of business life? If I solemnly promise to deliver the report by 5 pm on Friday, I will make sure it is delivered. This may sound trite, but the intent is to instill a greater sense of personal responsibility that has more weight and holds more respect for other people. If you make an agreement, feel it, believe it, and honor it. Then it becomes a covenant.

Speak your truth, face the facts

The second new gem of FACTS coaching is particularly directed at people who come from cultures in which politeness is important and saying what you really think is considered rude or offensive. As polite Englishmen, we are very familiar with this and often see people "go round the houses" and "dance round the handbags" rather than making an honest and direct point. They avoid entering the ZOUD.

Cultures like ours have a lot to learn from the likes of the Dutch and the Americans, who, on average, appear to be able to "hit the nail on the head" without being oversensitive to other people's reactions or feeling guilty for being direct. There is honesty in this level of directness that a coach can utilize, but in our experience this principle has been largely neglected in many coaching books, courses, and models.

You may be familiar with the story of the emperor's new clothes. In this well-known fable, the emperor was so taken by the charm of an unscrupulous tailor that he was persuaded to buy a suit of clothes that would be "invisible to anyone who was unfit for the emperor's position or just hopelessly stupid." The emperor could not see the cloth, but he did not wish to appear stupid and so agreed that the suit should be made. He paraded through the streets wearing the invisible suit—he was naked, but the crowd said nothing out of respect for the emperor and because they did not want to appear stupid. Suddenly a little boy, uninhibited by cultural politeness, spoke the truth: "The emperor has no clothes!" This Hans Christian Andersen story is over 150 years old, but it still has relevance today. If more people spoke their truth and faced the facts, wouldn't we have a much better business environment and society as a whole?

There is a significant connection here with coaching. Speaking your truth and facing the facts are key enablers of the transformation of both individuals and businesses. Coaches can lead the way by being role models, exemplifying this transformational behavior, and giving the coachee permission to practice direct and honest communication.

It is one thing to accept intellectually that speaking your truth and facing the facts is a necessary principle for FACTS coaching;

it is another to have the courage and skills to practice this on a daily basis. Whatever our cultural starting point, there is a fear of naming awkward truths and a temptation to avoid difficult conversations.

Certain characteristics, beliefs, and behaviors enable a challenging coach to speak their truth and face the facts. These include:

❏ Recognizing and accepting that everyone's truth is different and equally valid. This is based on perception, so we use the phrase "speaking *your* truth," not "speaking *the* truth."
❏ Having an instinct for the truth and being in touch with your emotions and intuition as an internal compass pointing to your truth.
❏ Being prepared to speak honestly, take risks, and challenge others, and to enter the ZOUD and hold people accountable for their actions.
❏ Stepping in on behalf of absent stakeholders and the common good and taking the risk of upsetting the status quo, not for personal gain but as a statement of your values, a daily proclamation of who you are.

Typical opening words you hear when a coach is speaking their truth are:

❏ "I have a gut feeling that..."
❏ "My instinct in this situation is..."
❏ "Don't ask me why but I have a hunch that..."
❏ "When you said that, the first thing that came into my head was..."
❏ "I keep getting this nagging thought that..."
❏ "I just had a flash of inspiration that..."

Facing the facts is different to speaking your truth, since it is an act of observation, perception, and reasoning. There is always a risk that you might be wrong, but if you are looking at the sky and it appears blue, then to you it is actually blue! So if you are looking at business performance figures that show performance is declining, it may be that it *is* declining. Just because the seven other people in your team are looking at the same figures and draw a different conclusion does not mean that it is not a fact.

You may be familiar with the 1957 film *Twelve Angry Men* starring Henry Fonda. It is a tense film set in the jury room in which 12 men deliberate the guilt or innocence of a young man accused of murder. In the United States the verdict must be unanimous, or the result is a hung jury and a mistrial. At the beginning of the film, the jurors vote on the guilt or innocence of the young man on the basis of reasonable doubt; the vote is 11 voting guilty, with Henry Fonda's character the lone voice maintaining that the boy is innocent. Over the course of the film's 96 minutes, Fonda's character speaks his truth, faces the facts, and convinces and persuades the other jurors that the boy is innocent. The film ends with a unanimous vote of innocent and the boy is acquitted. Sometimes the emperor really does not have any clothes and sometimes it falls to the coach to "say it as it is," even in the face of opposition and with the risk of appearing stupid or being ridiculed.

It should not surprise us that the "new gems" or columns of FACTS coaching are few in number and simple in theory. The challenge lies not in understanding the principles, but in putting them into practice on a daily basis amid the tensions of organizational life. The encouraging fact is that the more these principles are practiced, the easier they become. It is like exercising a neglected set of muscles in the gym. At first it is a struggle when your muscles ache and there is a great temptation to give up. But gradually you develop a new strength and what was once difficult and unnatural becomes routine and instinctive. We encourage you to practice, practice, practice in order to embed new habits based on these principles.

Self-evident truths

The nineteenth-century German philosopher Schopenhauer said: "All truth passes through three stages. First, it is ridiculed. Second, it is violently opposed. Third, it is accepted as being self-evident." In this book we speak our truth, which may be ridiculed and opposed by coaches immersed in traditional principles. However, we believe that the changes we advocate are necessary for coaching to expand its credibility as a developmental and business intervention directly linked to organizational effectiveness.

In this chapter we have looked at the evolution of coaching and its therapeutic origins. We challenged three principles of the traditional person-centered coaching approach: the false idols of the nondirective approach, holding to the individual's agenda, and building rapport. In their place, we have proposed five new columns supporting the FACTS coaching approach. We have rediscovered three hidden treasures that have been core to many coaching models and remain essential principles: passionate curiosity, trust in the future potential of all, and letting go of status and outcomes. In addition, we have identified the two new gems of build the contract, honor the contract and speak your truth, and face the facts.

In the next few chapters we look in detail at the skills involved in the FACTS coaching approach supported by these principles: Feedback, Accountability, Courageous goals, Tension, and Systems thinking. We identify high challenge/high support methods for ensuring that coaching maximizes its potential to facilitate organization-wide change on behalf of all business stakeholders.

CHAPTER 4
FACTS—Feedback

Be ready to transform but do not provoke, illuminate the darkness of ignorance but do not blind. (Tao Te Ching, Verse 58)

Executive coaches could use feedback more effectively—in particular, they could offer challenging feedback more often and to greater effect. A coach is in a privileged position and is a first-hand witness to a coachee's actions and words. We describe this as the "laboratory of learning," in which the coach makes observations and provides transformational feedback based on what they hear and see, and also on intuition. In this chapter we detail the components of effective feedback, using the support/challenge matrix to demonstrate the different levels and how high challenge and high support feedback can lead to transformation and peak performance. We also consider what holds us back from giving challenging feedback and the barriers preventing us using it to its full effect. As well as this person-centered approach, we also adopt the wider perspective of feedback relating to the team and the organization, taking in the view of other stakeholders.

Traditional feedback versus FACTS feedback

When researching the topic of feedback in coaching, we found a mix of coverage across the literature. Some coaching books do not mention feedback at all, others emphasize it. For example, in Laura Whitworth et al.'s *Co-Active Coaching* feedback is not explicitly mentioned, but the book refers to mirroring back what the coach hears and sharing observations as part of listening skills. *The Solutions Focus* by Paul Jackson and Mark McKergow discusses the role of reviewing what went well in "solutions mode," although it does not specifically talk about feedback. In *Coaching for Performance*, Sir John Whitmore details five levels of feedback, ranging from the unconstructive critical to a developmental coaching style. Furthermore, two of the largest coaching professional bodies have identified feedback as fundamental to the effectiveness of coaching. The International Coach Federation (ICF) identifies feedback as a core competence relating to direct communication, which mandates that a coach "is clear, articulate and direct in sharing and providing feedback." The Association for Coaching (AC) states that fostering independence in the coachee is a core competence; one of the three points within this is that "the coach monitors improvement in the coachee and feeds this back as evidence of development." However, offering challenging feedback appears to be seen as less important than and is hidden behind other more obvious coaching behaviors such as listening, questioning, establishing rapport, and goal setting. Why is this?

Some coaches consider that providing feedback is like giving advice and so it may be a directive step, preventing the coachee from having the opportunity to learn and seek feedback for themselves. Also, some coaches have told us they are worried that the feedback will be guided by the coach's agenda rather than the coachee's, and so it will be biased by the coach's perceptions, views, and experience. One experienced coach said, "I would only provide feedback if it was relevant." But how do you decide on relevance—except through value judgments by the coach?

We would say that in the laboratory of learning, everything is relevant. If the coach has seen, heard, thought, or felt something based on what a coachee has said or done while in the coaching session, it is disingenuous to hold back this information, otherwise the result may be continued habitual behavior and approaches that do not lead to the desired outcome.

Giving challenging feedback can provoke "identity issues" for the coach. It is core to the identity of most people who are attracted to coaching that they take pride in helping others to grow and develop. To risk upsetting the rapport in a relationship by providing challenging feedback threatens this self-view in a way that can feel acutely uncomfortable. In their book *Difficult Conversations*, Stone, Patton, and Heen say that the reason some conversations are so difficult for us is that "our anxiety results not just from having to face the other person but from having to face ourselves. The conversation has the potential to disrupt our sense of who we are in the world."

In order to give challenging feedback, the coach needs to be aware of any identity issues this might provoke—for example, "I am not the sort of person who makes other people get angry"— and not be in denial about the complexity and extent of such perceptions.

In the laboratory of learning a coachee experiments with new behaviors, reflecting on past experience and developing strategies, actions, and awareness that drive behavioral change. The coach interacts with the coachee and observes, reacts, has thoughts and feelings based on what the coachee has said or done, and thus forms hypotheses. The coach is a great source of feedback by providing information about how the coachee's action, words, tone of voice, and silences are interpreted. The assumption is that while in the coaching session, as long as there is a sufficient level of trust and rapport, the coachee displays behavior that is typical of how they behave outside of the coaching session when interacting with people on an everyday basis. If these assumptions are true, then the experiments and observations made in the laboratory of learning are valid and reliable as predictors. The coaching session cannot replicate every situation and so there are limitations, but on the whole this is a great source of information.

Levels of feedback:
Individual, team, and organizational

We can look at the impact of feedback and the effect of its absence using Johari's window, which was developed in 1955 by Joseph Luft and Harry Ingham, two psychologists researching group dynamics at the University of California, Los Angeles. The model describes the development of self-awareness by sharing information with other people and how feedback from others can help uncover blind spots, strengthen relationships, and build trust. Johari's window is depicted like a window with four panes of glass, as in the diagram opposite, but it is also a metaphorical window through which light can shine and provide insight, enabling a person to see something new by looking through it.

The vertical axis of Johari's window is "unknown to others" and "known to others," with the horizontal axis being "known to you" and "unknown to you." This produces a 2x2 matrix with four distinct panes.

The top left pane, "known by you, known by others," is called the *arena*, as everything is out in the open, everything here is seen and known, and it is in the public domain. You are conscious of your behavior and know what you have done, and other people know it too. In the diagram everyone knows that Lyn is wearing a black top: she put it on in the morning and everyone can see it. The top right pane is called the *blind spot*, "unknown to you, known to others." In the diagram, Lyn has white paint on the back of her black top that she cannot see and does not know about, but everyone else does. Bottom left is the pane "known to you,

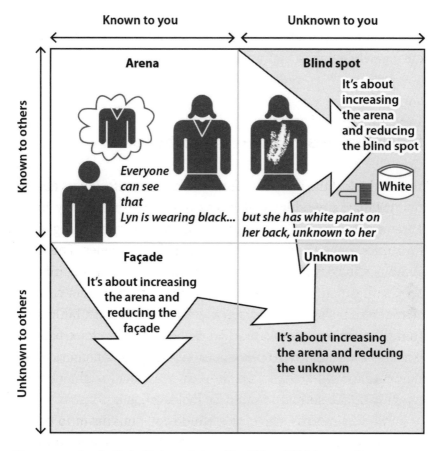

Diagram reproduced with the kind permission of Lyn Bicker of TSOC.

unknown to others," the *façade*, which represents things that are private and kept hidden from others. The final pane, bottom right, is the *unknown*, "unknown to you, unknown to others," where anything can be discovered but all is currently unknown.

The point of this model is to describe how self-awareness and trust can develop through interaction with other people. The arena is the pane that will lead to the greatest personal growth: relationships with other people will be strengthened through sharing and developing trust. This is not a static model, and by expanding the size of the arena, individuals and relationships can grow. By sharing private information about yourself, things that are hidden become known to other people, so the façade pane reduces and the arena expands. This can be done simply by talking about hobbies and interests, or where you went on holiday, and from this nonthreatening start building up to sharing thoughts, beliefs, and ideas, so that more of the whole you is known to other people. Others will then understand you more, they will be aware of your strengths and interests, and they will reciprocate and share more about themselves. This virtuous cycle builds trust and rapport.

The size of the arena can be expanded further by reducing blind spots, which is done through feedback. In our example, someone could tell Lyn that she had paint on her back, or in another situation Lyn could ask for feedback. In this way feedback is a gift, another pair of eyes to help people become aware of something that is out of sight. Awareness is the first stage of change: once you are aware of something you can choose to act, but if you are not aware there is no possibility of effective action leading to change.

It is relatively easy to offer feedback on people's strengths in order to decrease the size of the blind spot, and this is an important tool that a coach can use on a regular basis. People like to hear feedback about their strengths; it identifies hidden talents, builds confidence, and encourages further development. Consider the phrase "the ordinary is extraordinary." We take for granted what is normal and ordinary behavior for ourselves but may be extraordinary for other people. Examples could be drawing, riding a bike, or mental arithmetic. So feedback can help us understand our unique gifts, the strengths that set us apart from other people. Through this awareness we can focus on what we are good at, developing confidence in doing what comes naturally.

However, it is harder to give challenging feedback on topics about which the coachee may be in denial or which they may not wish to hear. If these topics are regarded as "no go" areas, the coach colludes in the restricted self-view that the coachee wishes to maintain. This is a particularly acute problem when working with confident, powerful business leaders with many people around them who think it is too risky to offer such feedback. How long will it be before these people get to hear other people's real perspectives and opinions?

Now consider team and organizational feedback. Just like individuals, teams have blind spots. At an organizational level, competitors look for organizational blind spots and try to fill these gaps to gain competitive advantage. Another perspective on corporate blind spots comes from psychologist Irving Janis, who in the 1970s coined the phrase "groupthink" to describe the thinking and decision-making processes within a group of people. He studied US foreign policy disasters, including the failure to identify the risk of a Japanese attack on Pearl Harbor in 1941 and the Cuban Bay of Pigs fiasco in 1961. Janis defined groupthink as "a mode of thinking that people engage in when they are deeply involved in a cohesive in-group, when the members' strivings for unanimity override their motivation to realistically appraise alternative courses of action."

The symptoms of groupthink are the minimization of conflict, self-censorship, and consensus being reached without critical evaluation or constructive debate. The result is a feeling of invulnerability. In practical terms this leads to incomplete consideration of alternative courses of action, failure to analyze risks, failure to gain an external perspective, poor data gathering, and a lack of contingency plans. A decision made in this environment is likely to be flawed because the cohesiveness of the group is more important. In the support/challenge matrix this certainly sounds like the "cosy club" of high support and low challenge, and in ZOUD terms there is a lack of uncomfortable debate in such a team. One way of preventing groupthink is to invite an external perspective, and this is the link back to coaching.

An anecdote illustrates this point from a different perspective. David and Jane were in a new relationship and had Sunday lunch together. Jane prepared a roast chicken, and David was curious to see her cut the legs off the chicken before putting it in the oven. Jane said she had been taught to cook chicken like that as it improved the flavor. The relationship developed and David was invited to Jane's parents for lunch. Jane's grandmother was also there, and David commented on the unusual way the family prepared roast chicken. The grandmother was surprised and said, "I can't believe she still cooks like that; I used to do that because our oven was so small that we had to cut the legs off to fit it in!"

Over time, the reason for a particular decision can be lost. Think about the organization you work in and the rituals that have developed over time that do not stand up to evaluation. Every organization has symbols, rituals, and cultural behavior that no longer add to its effectiveness. These rituals continue because there is no feedback and no questioning; there is an acceptance of the status quo and an absence of passionate curiosity. Another example is the banking crisis of 2008–09: in hindsight many analysts said the meltdown was inevitable and they could see what was going to happen. But why wasn't this spotted in foresight and not only in hindsight? When you have groupthink and blind spots, circumstances are accepted and not questioned and you have conformity and collusion.

Feedback and the support/challenge matrix

Most feedback falls into two quadrants of the support/challenge matrix: either the cosy club (high support, low challenge), which may be from a coach to a coachee; or stress (low support, high challenge) from a critical and status-conscious boss. The most effective feedback will be from high support, high challenge, which develops awareness and pushes the change that is necessary for future success.

Consider how often and in what situations you give and receive feedback. It may be praise from a loved one or friend, but most likely when feedback is forthcoming it is negative: feedback from a customer that the shipment was late, feedback for the boss that the project was over budget, feedback stored up until the annual appraisal meeting when it is presented out of context and detached from the event to which it relates. Often people view feedback as occurring only when something has gone wrong and there is a problem to correct. We presented our ideas of feedback to a group of 70 internal coaches with a large organization, and one of the audience said, "Once you have dumped all this feedback on the person, what are they meant to do?" They clearly did not see anything positive about feedback. So if on an individual level feedback is a great gift, why do we do it so infrequently, and when it is provided why is it delivered so badly?

In normal day-to-day interactions, there are many things that prevent effective feedback. Our experience of receiving negative feedback discourages us from offering even positive feedback. In addition, respect for the other person, not wishing to upset them, their status, relationship, organizational politics, and politeness may all result in feedback being edited or limited and so losing its value. Badly delivered feedback can be more harmful than no feedback at all. We can all think of something we said that was misinterpreted and taken as a negative comment, despite a heartfelt positive intention. Comments that are taken wrongly can lead to an emotional reaction that is very powerful. We are conscious that we do not wish to move into the stress quadrant of the support/challenge matrix, so we soften the message, which leads us to the cosy club. Because of this, over time feedback may not be sought out and may only be forthcoming when problems occur. A coach who holds the view that rapport is the number one priority will shy away from challenging feedback, as there is the risk that it leads to a breakdown in rapport and damages the coaching relationship irreparably.

Nevertheless, we strongly believe that in a coaching context feedback is valuable, as the coach is in a privileged and unique position:

❑ The coach is able to perceive and give feedback on what is said during the session, energy levels, avoidance, what is done between sessions, and so on.

❑ The coach is able to reflect on past events. The coachee may describe a situation and reflecting on the past can inform future actions. While exploring what happened and who said what, feedback can be used to provide an insight into what the coach heard and how they interpreted the actions, as well as asking the coachee if the possible interpretations had been considered and thinking about what to do in the future.

❑ The coach can help the coachee practice for the future. The coachee can be assisted in imagining a future situation through role playing or using an "empty chair" exercise. The coach can provide valuable input as the coachee rehearses new behaviors, like a theatrical director on stage working with an actor to perfect their performance.

Some coaches say to us that they provide feedback as an integral part of their work. However, when we have explored this in detail, it seems that the feedback is on a superficial level and comes from a nondirective, person-centered style that lacks depth and challenge. Feedback should have "bite," create insight, deliver a new perspective, and cause a step change. To explain this further, we can turn again to the support/challenge matrix and give example feedback for each quadrant.

Low support/low challenge
☐ "OK, and what happened next?"
☐ "Oh well, better luck next time."
☐ "I don't have any feedback, I have nothing to add."
☐ "Sometimes that's just the way business life is and you have to roll with it."

In the low support/low challenge quadrant, feedback is characterized as going through the motions, filling in time to the end of the meeting. Inertia and apathy rule and the coach's presence contributes little to the achievement of goals.

Low support/high challenge
☐ "Let me tell you something. We've had a couple of meetings now and you just don't seem to be getting to grips with this."
☐ "That was rubbish, my 5 year old could do better. Think harder!"
☐ "You expect me to accept that? That's not doing anything. Come on, you need to sharpen up!"
☐ "That's just an excuse. You're feeling sorry for yourself. Why can't you think outside of the box for a change like I demonstrated last time we met?"

In the bottom right quadrant challenge is high but support is low; the feedback is still ineffective, but stress is high. This is like a bullying line manager using their status to undermine a team member. There is a complete lack of understanding of the other person's perspective and no empathy, so the communication is very poor and will have a negative impact and further damage an already unhealthy relationship.

High support/low challenge

❑ "Don't believe what the board said, I think your project plan is very good. Maybe they were having a bad day."

❑ "That was very interesting and you're clearly energized by this subject."

❑ "It sounds like you dealt with that very skillfully."

❑ "Oh, well done, that was great!"

❑ "If you said that to me and I was one of your clients, I would be convinced."

❑ "I think you did very well in a difficult situation."

❑ "From what you said it sounds like you're a very effective communicator."

In the high support/low challenge quadrant there is a lot of positive affirmation: the coach actively boosts the coachee's ego and confidence through praise. It is our belief that much of the current coaching feedback lies in this area. Here the coach is overly focusing on positives and not always facing up to reality. The coach may be colluding with the coachee and accepting the status quo without challenge. The risk is that the feedback is irrelevant and out of touch.

High support/high challenge

❑ "I would like to give you some feedback. You talked about your assertiveness when with your boss. I've mentioned this three times today and each time you've changed the subject and talked about something else. What's happening here?"

❑ "You identified the objective of improving your impact and influence. I've noticed that every time you talk you look down at your notebook, and then there's no eye contact. At that point you lose impact."

❑ "I've noticed that your mobile phone keeps ringing and this is disrupting the flow of our conversation. I feel angry that this has happened a number of times and you haven't apologized for the interruption it has caused."

❑ "Your PA rang me to cancel our coaching session at three hours' notice. This is the second time this has happened and it makes me feel like this work isn't a priority for you right now."

The high support/high challenge quadrant is built on the quality of the relationship between two people: the higher the level of trust, the higher the potential impact of challenging feedback. Coaching feedback should be challenging and supportive, and more challenging as the coaching relationship develops—this is the difference between "normal" feedback and FACTS feedback. This is speaking your truth and facing the facts. We would say that the quality of feedback is directly correlated to the strength of the relationship on the depth of trust, as displayed in the diagram overleaf.

A good coach is in touch with their instincts, creating hypotheses and intuitively testing these out through feedback and statements. The challenging coach is willing to take risks: risking rapport to enter the ZOUD in the search for an answer and a long-term sustained change.

Giving challenging feedback: Individual level

So for feedback to be as effective as possible, it must be founded on a strong relationship in which both challenge and support are high. While there have been a number of books touching on these skills, they tend to be related to mediation skills rather than coaching skills. For example, *Difficult Conversations* by Bruce Patton, Douglas Stone, and Sheila Heen and *Fierce Conversations*

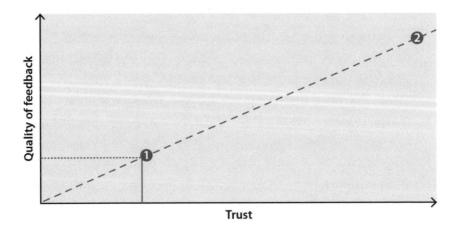

Quality of feedback (y-axis)

Trust (x-axis)

❶ The cosy club
Some trust, but limited feedback, which tends only to be positive out of fear of breaking rapport and permanently damaging the relationship.

❷ High challenge, high support
The relationship is very strong with a lot of trust, so both parties can say anything knowing it will be respected and the relationship will not be damaged.

by Susan Scott provide excellent approaches suited to mediation or negotiation. We have built on these models to produce an approach specifically for coaching, which ensures that high support, high challenge feedback is delivered as effectively as possible in a coaching context. Our model has six stages:

1   *Observation*—what was seen/what happened? This is a specific and factual description that is nonjudgmental. This is just how it is, and is formed from the coach's view of the "act," not the "actor." For example, in each of the last two sessions John has not completed the actions he said he would.

2   *Preparation and opening statement*—the first words spoken are the most important, so preparation and practice are crucial. To do this, the coach can write down an opening statement and practice saying it out loud. The opening statement should name the issue, and contain specific examples from

the observations in Stage 1 that illustrate the matter at hand.

3   *Impact*—describe the emotional and business impact that the issues cause for you or for other stakeholders. What assumptions did you (or others) make as a result? How did you feel? What are the consequences? This is about bringing the coach's presence into the laboratory of learning, and the coach speaking their truth and facing the facts. Some nondirective or person-centered coaches would say that the perception of the coach is irrelevant, as these feelings, thoughts, and perceptions are from the coach and not related to the coachee's agenda. However, if we assume that the coach is a typical person, then the perceived impact will also be typical and have a similar impact when replicated outside the laboratory of learning.

An example of an opening statement incorporating Stages 1, 2, and 3 is:

> COACH: John, I want to raise with you the topic of your time management. The last two times we've met you've been over 15 minutes late for the meeting. I feel frustrated about this behavior and am worried that I will conclude you aren't committed to this work, and then I won't make it a priority to focus on it going forward. I also recall that in your 360° feedback report your line manager scored you low in this area, so I wonder whether my own frustration is also mirrored by others in the organization. This could jeopardize your prospects of securing the promotion you've identified as your next goal.

4   *Invite input and listen*—now that the coach has shared their perception, there is the opportunity to explore the shared

reality: "Is what I heard the same as what you said?" or "Did you intend what you said to be interpreted as I did?" A simple way of doing this is: "How do you see this?" "What is your take on this situation?" At this point, the coach relies on the traditional coaching skills of listening and powerful questions to dig for as full an understanding from the coachee's perspective as possible. The coach listens for words and tone, observes body language, and is perceptive to feelings. Through paraphrasing, summarizing, and reflecting, the coach ensures that the coachee has been heard and their opinion acknowledged. This is an honest sharing of perceptions rather than an argument that needs to be won or a position that needs to be justified. The coach works hard to assume a nondefensive position and to detach from their personal interest in the situation.

5 *Reflection*—if this is a significant issue, then allow time for both parties to reflect; give it the "24-hour test." Allow the coachee 24 hours to reflect and contemplate the matter rather than force a resolution. Often in the moment of feedback emotions can take over and may be too strong to allow clarity of thought. In a busy world we often rush quickly toward action that may not be best in the long term when navigating sensitive topics.

6 *Action*—what should be done? Feedback is only useful if it can be used to change something and so is future focused and constructive. If this isn't the case, we question why the feedback has been provided and what motivated the intervention. A future focus can be achieved by simply asking: "What can you do to change this?" "How can we move forward from here given our new understanding?" "What is our new agreement and how will we honor this together?" The action may be agreed after a period of reflection.

As can be seen from the above approach, an important aspect of giving challenging feedback effectively is preparation: preparing what to feed back and how to maximize its impact. It is the same with any new skill, such as learning to drive a car: practice is needed. As we learn any skill we go through four stages: unconscious incompetence (we don't know what we don't know, and don't understand why things aren't working), conscious incompetence (our awareness has developed and we now know why something isn't right, but we don't know what to do to fix it), conscious competence (we now know what to do and we can do it), and unconscious competence (we are skilled and can do it without thinking). To explain the unconscious competence stage, think about the metaphor of driving a car: you may have had an uneventful journey home and thought "How did I get here?" as the process of driving has become so natural that it did not require any conscious effort. Through practice, giving challenging feedback can reach the same level of unconscious competence and feedback becomes more natural. The preparation you need may be just a couple of seconds of mental rehearsal.

The above process also demonstrates that in the laboratory of learning, as well as coachees learning from the feedback, coaches will also learn and should expect to receive challenging feedback themselves. In fact, good coaches should actively seek and welcome feedback as part of their continuing development. It could be said that before we are ready and able to give feedback, we must be able to receive it—only then can we appreciate how it feels and be ready to give feedback based on experience and knowledge. We need to be able to role model receiving feedback in a positive way.

Giving challenging feedback:
Team and organizational level

As we mentioned earlier, feedback in coaching has traditionally been person centered. This limits the potential of the coaching work to have an impact on the wider team and organization. The move beyond a person-centered stance involves a more intimate involvement in the coaching process of other organizational stakeholders, whether those be line managers, team peers, customers, mentors, or board sponsors. It also requires the coach to have a more intimate knowledge of the business, its sector, and leadership best practice in general. While, to some extent, the coach can research this knowledge before an engagement with a new organization, the effectiveness of team and organizational feedback will be maximized if the coach has operated as a leader in a similar environment. This challenges the notion that it is not necessary for a coach to have had business leadership experience. To clarify, we are not talking about mentoring, but asserting that for coaches to coach business executives there needs to be a common lexicon based on experience.

Ultimately, this is an issue of intuition and confidence. Through working in business over many years, a leader accrues a body of understanding that becomes unconscious and automatic. For a coach, this generates confidence in navigating the coachee's world and triggers intuition when listening to their challenges and goals. A coach who has experience of the business world will also empathize quickly with the views of other stakeholders and anticipate their likely questions, challenges, and opinions. Don't use this empathy and knowledge to take a judgmental stance, but don't lose the opportunity to make a healthy challenge either.

For example, we work with many clients using 360° feedback tools at the start of a coaching program to gather the perceptions of other stakeholders. The feedback report is valuable to an extent on its own, but quantitative scores on a feedback chart are often only the tip of the iceberg in terms of the value that can be gained by a business-savvy coach. The devil is often in the detail of the minor differences and "shades of gray" in such reports. Similarly, stakeholder interviews are frequently used as part of the contracting phase in setting up a coaching assignment. In discussions with the business sponsors, line manager, and HR representatives, the coach needs to be adept at grasping the wider context in which personal change will support team and organizational goals. This is an understanding often driven by the nature of the questions that coach asks, which come from their personal organizational experience.

In order to bring the concept of team and organizational feedback to life in a more practical fashion, consider the following examples, each taken from a different quadrant of the support/ challenge matrix:

Low support/low challenge

- ❑ "I mentioned to your line manager that it is not realistic for us to define 'bottom-line' impacts for this work, since these are notoriously difficult to measure."
- ❑ "I am not a business expert and I really want to focus on your personal behavior and what drives this."
- ❑ "I respect your desire not to involve your line manager in the final review of our work and trust this is the right way to go."
- ❑ "It really surprised me that you've been removed from your position, since I thought you were making great progress toward your goals."

Low support/high challenge

- ❑ "Your boss has told me that you need to buck your ideas up or you will struggle to keep your job."

❑ "In the contracting conversation your HR manager was struggling to see how you could resolve this situation and I tend to agree."

❑ "I notice that shares in your company have dropped 60 percent over the past 12 months. Are you worried that you could default on your bank loans?"

❑ "Yes, I've seen this all before. You're being set up as the fall guy for the recent poor performance of the widgets division and it is because you are politically naïve."

High support/low challenge

❑ "Your 360° feedback report shows that you are very highly regarded in the area of commercial expertise and client relationships."

❑ "From my review with your team members, the customer service levels you have achieved in the last quarter are exceptional. You must be proud of this achievement."

❑ "I noticed in our contracting conversation that you and your line manager have a great working relationship. It was obvious that he holds you in high regard, particularly when he was talking about the staff survey results."

❑ "I know there has been a major drive in this organization to reduce its carbon footprint. I think you could use your work in reducing waste in the plant as a great example of this."

High support/high challenge

❑ "I took a look at your company accounts and I noticed that the CEO is focusing on increasing customer service levels this year. What is the impact of this on your own goals?"

❑ "A word I notice a number of your 360° respondents have used in your feedback is 'visible.' This also makes me think of your line manager's request that you take a more visible role in the business going forward. This word 'visible' crops up a lot. What do you make of that?"

❑ "In the interviews I conducted with your direct reports, more than once I came across a perception that you were considered distant and aloof. Have you encountered this perception before?"

❑ "Reading between the lines of what your line manager was saying in the contracting discussion, it sounds to me that he has a very different view of the goals for this coaching work than you or I do. Is this true?"

❑ "If I was one of the company's shareholders and I was listening to what you just said, I think I would give you the following feedback..."

A coach is well placed to cut through cultural rituals that have developed over time. They are detached from the team and organization and not interested in group cohesiveness, so immune to the contagion of groupthink. A coach can declare that the "emperor has no clothes" without fear of ridicule. The very nature of the external perspective allows organizational assumptions to be validated in an objective way. The coach is free to speak their truth and face the facts. As soon as they walk through the doors of the organization the coach is in the laboratory of learning, and can observe how they were greeted at reception, what the atmosphere is like in the staff coffee shop, and what posters or notices are on display. The coach can play devil's advocate, a valuable process in provoking depth of thought to ensure that decisions and actions represent the long-term interest of the individual, team, and wider organization.

Of course, team and organizational feedback may often involve giving challenging feedback to other stakeholders who are involved in the coaching process. In a contracting conversation or a review meeting, coaches may find themselves giving upward feedback to boardroom sponsors or line managers in situations where there is a fixed view of the world that the coach's own perspective does not support. Over time, the coach builds a body of understanding of the culture, politics, and business context of the overall company, which allows them to give nonpersonalized feedback on the general trends and patterns they are experiencing in their coaching work. These viewpoints can be a valuable "early warning" system for the organization regarding future opportunities and threats, and allow the coach to add more value to the organization as a whole.

Our model for giving challenging feedback to individuals can also be used when providing team and organizational feedback. Imagine the following as a prepared opening statement to a company CEO who has just sponsored a nine-month talent-development program for his top 20 executives. The situation is a one-to-one conversation at the end of the program to review progress, outcomes, and next steps:

> COACH: Anne, I want to raise with you the topic of your leadership culture. In the coaching conversations I have had with your executives, a number of times different individuals have said that there is no recognition of success in the company and that this is a missed opportunity in terms of raising morale and staff engagement. I'm worried this may be a factor in the rising attrition levels in your middle management population. With the improving market in your sector this trend may get worse over the coming months if your competitors "cherry pick" your top talent. In hindsight, I would have made this aspect a more significant part of the talent-development program, for example holding

some dinners hosted by board members where individual and team success on the program could have been recognized publicly. What is your view on this?

Once again, this kind of feedback can provoke an emotional response and break rapport in the short term. If it is a topic others have not felt able to raise with the CEO, there will be a good reason for this! However, once any storm has passed it is likely that such interventions will succeed in building trust and in delivering results.

We would like to "turn up the volume" on feedback in coaching. We believe it has not taken its proper place among the other important coaching skills. We have therefore proposed two shifts: toward high challenge, high support feedback, and from a person-centered perspective to a team and organizational perspective. In each area we have explored how challenging feedback is best delivered so that it is an essential element for effective coaching in a business environment. Coaches are uniquely positioned to role model how this is done with both courage and compassion.

EXERCISE

This exercise is an opportunity to practice giving feedback. Work with a colleague and consider this as a coaching session. You are coaching someone who wants to achieve the goal of throwing a small ball over their shoulder so that it lands in a trash can 6 feet behind them. Observe as your colleague throws the ball over their shoulder into the trash can, and prepare and then provide feedback. Work through the stages:

1   **Observation**—mentally note what was seen/what happened, practice being as specific and precise as possible by making a note of what happened and the end result.

2   **Preparation and opening statement**—write down the first sentence you are going to say, and mentally rehearse changing the emphasis and intonation. What is the feeling you want to convey: praise, challenge, support?

3   **Impact**—write down all the possible assumptions that you (or someone else) could make. Be realistic and then wild and extreme and list as many emotional responses as you can think of.

Now say what you have prepared based on Stages 1, 2, and 3. For example: "The ball landed 2m to the left, and before that you were 1m to the right and 2m left the time before that. You seem to be repeating the same mistakes. I wonder if you are really trying!"

4   **Invite input**—"How do you see this?" Step outside of the exercise and ask your colleague what they thought and felt about your feedback, how specific it was, whether it could be more challenging, and so on. (The coachee provides feedback on your feedback.)

5   **Reflection**—does your coachee need time to reflect? Give them the opportunity to do this if required.

6   **Action**—what should be done? Keep this future focused and constructive (something can be done). For example, "Keep your arm straight and release the ball when your arm touches your ear."

Repeat the steps above until your coachee succeeds in throwing the ball into the bin (or for a maximum of five throws). Each time increase the challenge, "turn up the volume," and observe what is happening for you and the other person in the laboratory of learning.

FACTS example dialogue

David is a senior manager with a large organization. As part of a large-scale leadership-development program, David is receiving five two-hour coaching sessions. The purpose of the coaching is to embed the learning from the taught elements of the program and to personalize the work so that it focuses on David's key areas of development. The contracting process has taken place and personal development objectives have been agreed between David, his line manager, and the human resources director.

The prime area that David has identified for his development is influence and impact. As he put it, he wants to "establish himself as a respected member of the team, be recognized as an expert and be well informed, with a sensible viewpoint, in one-to-one discussions and in meetings." David listed the measures of success for this objective as "people taking on board what I say, that I come across as confident when conveying opinions and points of view, and there is an increase in the number of people asking for my advice and opinion."

David is an experienced and intelligent person and during the discussions it is evident that his style when communicating has a significant impact on his ability to be seen as confident and persuasive. When David talks he always looks down at his notepad on the desk and does not make any eye contact at all. The volume of his voice reduces and at times it is difficult to hear what he is saying. This occurs throughout the first meeting as rapport is built and his development objectives are worked through in detail.

It is now the second coaching meeting. We are back in the laboratory of learning as the coach develops hypotheses to test out in the coaching session. The key is for the coach to prepare and do some scenario planning. The hypotheses could be:

- ❑ This may be a product of the first coaching session and not typical of David's everyday style.
- ❑ This is typical and so the coach should be prepared to provide David with feedback.

For each hypothesis, the coach has prepared an opening sentence.

The second meeting starts as the first meeting ended. David's communication style is exactly the same: he looks down every time he talks and it is difficult to hear him. The coach concludes that the second hypothesis is correct. Once David has reported on progress on the actions he agreed at the first meeting, the coach reviews the objectives to check relevance and find out whether priorities have changed.

David confirms that influencing and communication are still at the heart of his areas for development and this provides the coach with the link to provide feedback on what has been observed.

The FACTS Response

COACH: You identified the objective of improving your impact and influence and I would like to give you some feedback. I've noticed that every time you talk you look down at your notebook, and then there is no eye contact. When you do this I can't hear you very well, the energy level seems to drop, I feel that you may not be confident about what you are saying, and what you are saying loses impact. What do you think about my assumption?

[This is a clear statement of fact without judgment.]

COACHEE: I agree with what you say and I know I do this. If this is what you've noticed, I guess other people will as well. I guess this is a significant thing for me to change if I want to influence people and communicate with influence."

[The coachee is aware and motivated to take action. He knows about a blind spot and wants to take action to change. The benefit to him is the achievement of his goal, which is to be noticed.]

> COACH: Let's try an exercise. Talk to me for five minutes about your most recent holiday and maintain eye contact as you speak.

[The coachee talks freely in the safe environment of the coaching room and accepts the challenge. However, he still looks down at his notebook even though there is nothing written on the open pages. The coach reaches over and takes the notebook away, closes it, and puts it on the other side of the table. The coachee smiles as he recognizes why the coach has done this and continues talking for four minutes. The coach pauses the exercise.]

> COACH: How was that?

[A detailed conversation follows, with great openness and depth of thought from David. An action plan is agreed and the session ends. During this coaching session the coachee received feedback and challenge. The "elephant in the room" was identified and awareness and action followed. Through preparation by the coach, the feedback was constructive and future focused. The coachee faced the FACTS and has started to move on. The coach can continue to challenge the coachee to face the habits that are holding him back from achieving the goals he desires.

CHAPTER 5

FACTS—Accountability

*Be firm and armed but do no harm, be as sharp as a knife
but do not cut. (Tao Te Ching, Verse 58)*

Next in our understanding of the FACTS approach is "A"
for accountability. What we mean by accountability can be
defined as "the obligation of an individual, firm, or institution
to account for its activities, accept responsibility for them, and
disclose the results in a transparent manner." In this chapter we
explain the difference between ordinary levels of accountability in
coaching and FACTS levels of accountability. We use the support/
challenge matrix to explore specific accountability interventions,
and assess the impact of these and the circumstances in which
each might be effective.

The rising tide of accountability

To understand the role of accountability in the FACTS approach it
is important to reflect on the wider attitude toward accountability
in society at large. Recent events such as the public reaction to the
UK parliamentary expenses scandal, the backlash from the US
public and politicians to the BP Florida oil spill, and the global
sense of disgust at the financial industry bonus culture suggest
that there is a shift in attitudes in the wider world. What trends
are driving this change?

Technology and the internet are making information more
freely available to a global audience in an uncensored format. In
parallel, Generation Y is growing up with a less deferent attitude

to those in authority: they are less likely to give people respect based on a job title alone and they have higher expectations of standards of behavior in institutions.

When these trends are combined with a severe economic recession, then public tolerance for excess, greed, elitism, and privilege reaches a new low. Take the example of the parliamentary expenses scandal in the UK. The vast majority of MPs had not done anything illegal, or even broken any policy rule, yet still the public vented unprecedented anger on those they saw as failing to meet their accountability as public servants. The public expected each individual to apply their own moral code. Few passed this test and, as a result, the public lost further respect for this brand of leader.

Similarly, when BP found itself in the midst of the Florida oil spill crisis, CEO Tony Hayward found himself at the center of a political storm when his casual comments about "wanting his life back" provoked fury among those whose livelihoods were threatened by what they saw as his company's mistakes. At the subsequent congressional inquiry he was accused of "stonewalling" and "kicking the can down the street" as he struggled to account for the circumstances that led up to the disaster and tried to distance himself personally from the chain of events. Again, this incident sent a loud message to those in positions of power in business that the government and the public at large expect much greater levels of accountability than has previously been the case.

This rise in demands for accountability around the world is creating a new and more challenging environment for business leaders, who feel that the goalposts are moving in terms of what is expected of them in both their personal and professional lives. Following the global recession and in an age of business renewal, every business requires more from every person within it and each person is held accountable to ever more stringent criteria. Leaders are being required to demonstrate greater levels of transparency in all of their dealings. They also need to build and maintain a personal code of ethics that sets an example to those they lead and can survive the relentless scrutiny of aggressive shareholders and wider stakeholders.

Levels of accountability in coaching

Executive coaches are also not immune from this trend and need to ask themselves: "What is our best role as agents of account-ability as we support and challenge the business leaders we work with?" and "How do we anticipate the future trend of ris-ing accountability and role model this in our work with business leaders to create the conditions for them to reach their highest potential?" Sometimes when we have discussed this topic with our peers in the coaching world, we have met with a response such as: "Yes, accountability. We know all about that. We're doing it already. You're not telling us anything new." It is true that all coaches work with accountability at some level or another. But the environment has changed and will continue to demand a greater level of focus on leadership accountability in particular.

In our work we have experienced three levels at which the coach can act as an agent of accountability, as in the diagram oppo-site. Level 1 accountability is focused on the personal actions, learn-ing, and alignment of the coachee, for example asking a coachee:

- ❑ "How did you get on with the actions you took from our last meeting?"
- ❑ "So what have you learned from that experience?"
- ❑ "I notice that what you are saying now contradicts how you behaved in our last meeting. What is going on here?"

Levels of accountability

Personal

Contract and coach

Organization

These questions limit the concept of accountability to the individual sphere of responsibility, regardless of the individual's role in the business and their relationship with the coach.

In Level 2 accountability, the coach also holds the coachee accountable to the coaching contract they have agreed and to the relationship they are building with the coach. For example, the coaching agreement may state that coaching sessions canceled at less than three working days' notice will incur a cancellation fee. When the coach holds the coachee accountable to this, they are not just protecting their own business model, they are holding the coachee accountable for the impact of their behavior on other people. If a coachee is always canceling sessions at short notice, it is likely that this is also happening in relation to other agreements and commitments with others in the workplace. Being held accountable to the consequences of this behavior is critical in raising their self-awareness. How many people around a powerful business leader may be letting this go and putting up with it for a quiet life? Does this serve their development as leaders?

The coaching agreement will also contain the expectations of other stakeholders. For example, if a line manager expects that the coachee "ups their game" in the area of focus and prioritization, this goal will have been captured in the coaching agreement before the start of coaching. In the midst of a subsequent coaching session, the coach may hold them accountable to this by saying: "I'm finding that we're jumping from one issue to the next and I'm getting confused as to what your priority for this coaching is. This reminds me of the expectations of your line manager in the coaching contract. I think we should take a step back here and imagine what she would be making of this conversation." In a sense, Level 2 accountability, when contracted appropriately, enables the coach to hold the coachee accountable to the voice of the stakeholders represented in that contract, who will often be a line manager, an HR representative, internal mentors, and the coach. It is a powerful perspective for the coach to represent and the development of a sophisticated upfront coaching contract is an essential prerequisite to working in this way.

Level 3 accountability takes this a stage further and happens when the coach chooses to act as an agent of accountability for the voice of unrepresented stakeholders in the wider system. What does this mean? Whatever is written in a coaching agreement, a coachee is accountable to their role in their organization with its many stakeholders, including customers, suppliers, staff, shareholders, and the public at large. The coachee is also acting as a business leader, a professional occupation with certain ethics, responsibilities, and best-practice ways of working. In Level 3 accountability the coach holds the coachee accountable to these hidden stakeholders and to these unwritten standards of professional conduct. Their purpose in so doing is to seek a win/win outcome for all stakeholders, rather than optimizing the outcome for the coachee and risking a negative impact elsewhere in the organization. At Level 3 the coach is focusing on the wider potential of the overall organizational context, not that of the individual alone.

It is essential for the FACTS coach to be experienced in the world of business and business leadership if they are to be credible and skillful, holding the coachee to this level of accountability. This is because they are required to imagine what the situation may look like from other stakeholders' perspectives and to challenge the coachee based on their own understanding of what constitutes business best practice. Example interventions at Level 3 are:

❑ "In my knowledge of this organization, your strategy is to innovate in the market. How is your response to this situation honoring that strategy?"

❑ "In my experience in business, best practice in this area would be to brief all of your team on the upcoming changes. What is your reason for not doing this?"

❑ "I notice in your annual accounts that one of this company's values is honesty. How could this value help you in this situation?"

❑ "What do you think your staff would make of this decision, given that you have recently announced a pay freeze throughout the organization?"

Skilled coaches work at all three levels of accountability, seamlessly moving from one to another according to the situation. They recognize that each level is crucial yet different.

We worked with a leading global travel company where accountability was identified as the key focus for an organization-wide culture-change program. The background was that the company was uncompetitive in its sector and had many outdated working practices and policies. Unfortunately, the knock-on effect was that the company was unable to make a profit and meet the expectations of another stakeholder group, namely the shareholders. As tension rose during an economic downturn, the leaders of the organization decided that the situation was unsustainable and challenged employees to step up to a greater level of accountability for performance and change. The employee groups were represented by trade union bodies, which immediately perceived the challenge as an unfair attack on a hard-working and stressed workforce. A full-blown industrial dispute ensued, costing the employees and the company many millions of pounds of lost income and revenue.

There were many times when the courage and resolve of this organization's leaders were tested to breaking point. Many of them wondered whether the degree of confrontation, aggravation, and challenge was worth it at a personal level. Of course, at times some doubted whether what they were doing was right and whether the situation could have been guided down a more peaceful path. While we cannot know how the situation would have been different without coaching support using the FACTS approach, it is our strong intuition that a purely person-centered approach would have tempted all parties to focus on their own interests, behaviors, and feelings, as opposed to holding them accountable to the facts and the truth of the wider situation; that is, that the company's commercial viability was under threat if they were not prepared collectively to step into the ZOUD and negotiate on an adult-to-adult basis. As coaches, we trust that in a small yet significant way our behavior role modeled all three levels of accountability and provided personal examples of the difficult conversations that are sometime unavoidable when the stakes are this high.

Coaching the CEO: An accountability dilemma

To understand how levels of accountability work alongside the support/challenge matrix, we can conduct a simple thought experiment. It is 2006 and you are the coach to the leader of one of the major banks that were to collapse in the "credit crunch" of 2007–09. You have been contracted to coach this CEO for six sessions of two hours and you are about to start the second session at his luxurious and intimidating offices in central London. This coaching session happens to coincide with the day that the bank's share price reaches its peak in the boom; happy days! The CEO arrives for the session a fashionable ten minutes late and looks to you to take the lead.

"How have you got on with the actions you committed to take from our first coaching session?" you venture boldly.

"Could you just remind me what those actions were?" he replies.

"Well, you were going to speak to your HR director to review the bonus scheme for senior managers."

"Look, I've been rather busy," he replies sharply. "I've been tied up with some really important pension negotiations and I haven't had the time to do any of those actions."

As the coach, what would you do now?

In front of you is the chief executive of one of the most powerful organizations in the world. The organization is paying you a princely sum to coach him. Part of you is screaming to let it go and not risk the rapport and relationship you have so carefully been building. This is partly because you believe this is good coaching and partly because you have a lot to lose if you upset this CEO, such as your reputation, your fees, and your prospect of any future work in the account. Another part of you is urging you to be brave and hold him accountable, to explore the precedent that is being set and not to become just another fawning acolyte. You're wishing you'd been more explicit about accountability in your initial contracting session with him. Where do you turn for help? Keeping in mind the three levels of accountability, what level of accountability would you hold him to in this situation? Would your response be any different if you knew that in six months' time your coachee will be featured all over the newspapers, pilloried for everything that is wrong in the financial services sector and for having brought the company to its knees?

Revisiting the support/challenge matrix

The support/challenge matrix we introduced earlier generates various options that might be used to respond as a coach in this situation. All of these options would meet one or more of the various recognized coaching competencies. However, using the FACTS approach, we can surmise that the coach would be working with accountability in the high support/high challenge quadrant of the model and holding accountability at all three levels: personal, contract/relationship, and system. In the good times, maybe we are tempted to accept our coachees and their failings too easily, to "meet them where they are at" and take the path of least resistance by giving them some slack and letting go. While these skills remain part of the experienced coach's toolkit, the FACTS

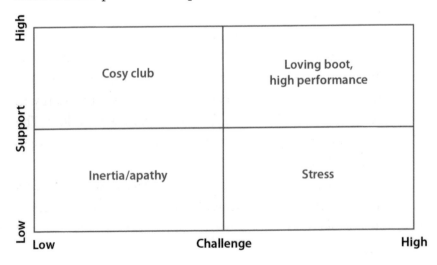

coach operating in an age of business renewal shifts the balance and acts with courage to hold the most senior leaders accountable with the "loving boot" if this is what the situation calls for.

Low challenge/low support

What does this look like in practice? Returning to our thought experiment, we can first explore what it doesn't look like via example interventions from other quadrants of the support/challenge matrix.

First, in the low challenge/low support quadrant, example responses to the CEO's statement might be:

- ❏ "OK, so what do you want to focus on for today's meeting?"
- ❏ "Tell me some more about what you've done since we last met."
- ❏ "What is the general situation in the business right now?"

A low challenge/low support intervention tends to have the following characteristics: matter-of-fact, changing the topic, no empathy or sense of care, a sense of small talk and superficiality. The coach is going through the motions with a blind acceptance of what the coachee says. These interventions are in the zone of comfortable debate. What impact are they likely to have on a busy, results-oriented, and driven CEO? The honest answer is very little. This type of individual has not engaged you to indulge in small talk. What are the risks of this approach? Immediately, the energy in this conversation will drop and the connection will be lost. The CEO fixes you with a stare and fears that this coaching is going to be predictable, boring, and very safe.

Typically, CEOs are paid to make decisions quickly based on minimal information and a lot of gut instinct. In this situation, you are likely to find that the coaching engagement ends prematurely. At best, the CEO is honest with you and gives you feedback from which you can learn. At worst, you find that he is too busy to turn up for future sessions and the relationship ends by default, leaving you confused about why the outcome was not a better one for all parties involved.

You know you have hit the low support/low challenge quadrant when:

❑ The energy drops.
❑ The connection is lost.
❑ The conversation is predictable and boring.
❑ The conversation does not deepen or become more personal.
❑ The conversation ends prematurely.

Low challenge/high support

Example responses from this quadrant would be:

❑ "What sort of busy is too busy?"
❑ "It sounds like you've had a difficult few weeks. How does that make you feel?"
❑ "You must be used to the goalposts shifting in your role. How do you cope with that?"

In many a textbook, these would be regarded as typical nondirective coaching responses, since they meet the criteria of many coaching competencies:

❑ Focus on the individual, their thoughts, feelings, and behavior.
❑ Use of nonjudgmental, open questions.
❑ Reflecting back and paraphrasing to create empathy.
❑ A sense of genuine personal care.
❑ Holding to the individual's agenda.

They would also be typical responses in a therapeutic session when a counselor is working with a fragile and troubled patient who has little self-esteem and needs great care and support to make even the smallest step forward. Our CEO is not a fragile individual by any stretch of the imagination! He is a confident, driven achiever who boldly sets ambitious visions and fights market competition with abandon and glee.

So while none of these responses is wrong in coaching terms, the better question is whether they are effective. What is their impact in this situation with this individual? If answered genuinely, these questions will raise the CEO's self-awareness. Their eyes will lift to the ceiling and they will dig deeper to find answers. These interventions demonstrate clearly that the coach is curious about the CEO's thinking and being in a way that will develop rapport and trust over time in this relationship. The personal connection will strengthen and the conversation will start to flow; sometimes in a way that makes it difficult to find an appropriate point to end.

It is great to be on the receiving end of low challenge/high support interventions and the individual can benefit greatly from this type of coaching. However, the real problem with the low challenge/high support stance is that it is entirely focused on Level 1 accountability at best. In some cases there could be no accountability at all, with every missed action, every inconsistent word/behavior, and every missed appointment ignored in order not to risk breaking rapport with the individual. Ultimately, with no accountability at all, the CEO loses respect for the coach and the relationship ends. Even at Level 1 accountability, where the coach expects accountability to personal actions, consistency of words and behavior, and responsibility for personal learning, the potential impact of the coaching intervention will be restricted to the development of improved personal effectiveness, independent of the wider expectations of other stakeholders and of the bottom-line performance of the business.

Many coaches have had the unsettling experience of working with an individual on a personal agenda, observing them make great progress, and then finding out six months later that they have left the role because they were not regarded as being effective from the organizational perspective. In these situations, the coach has colluded with the individual agenda in a fashion that has not served the goals of the organization. This style of coaching encourages a degree of self-obsession that can blind the coach and the coachee to the wider truth of the situation. Ultimately, it is always the will of the organization and the wider system that prevails. While it is appropriate to start with low challenge/high support interventions at the beginning of the coaching relationship in order to build trust, it soon becomes a limited and unsustainable style when working in an organizational setting with senior leaders.

You know you've hit the low challenge/high support quadrant when:

- ❑ The coachee demonstrates leaps in self-awareness.
- ❑ The coachee trusts you and starts to open up at a deeper level.
- ❑ The coachee's eyes shift to the ceiling as they dig deeper into themselves.
- ❑ The personal connection between coach and coachee strengthens.
- ❑ It is difficult to bring the meeting to an end!
- ❑ You gradually lose touch with the organizational context of the coaching.
- ❑ All parties enjoy the conversations but are less clear about the results they have delivered.

❏ You don't have the time or the will to check back to the original coaching contract to evaluate outcomes and impacts beyond the subjective impressions of the coachee.

High challenge/low support

The high challenge/low support quadrant is the domain of a command-and-control style of leadership. Example coaching interventions would be:

❏ "Whose time are we wasting here?"
❏ "You're clearly not committed to this coaching, so why don't we end it now?"
❏ "Do you have a reputation for not carrying through on your commitments?"
❏ "You CEOs are all the same. You're quick to tell others what to do, but when it comes to your own commitments you don't follow through at all."
❏ "This is just not good enough."

You know you've hit the high challenge/low support spot when:

❏ The coachee sits up straight, raises their eyebrows, and opens their eyes wide.
❏ The individual laughs, gets angry, or starts justifying themselves.
❏ The rapport in the relationship is broken, either temporarily or permanently.
❏ You feel your blood pressure rising and your palms sweating.

These responses would be amusing if they were not very common when used, not typically by coaches, but by experienced leaders who sometimes still regard being in the high challenge/low support space as some sort of badge of honor, an entitlement that comes from being the boss. Of course, when combined with a position of authority and power, the high challenge/low support quadrant is the home of the bully. At its extreme, it is an approach that results in abuse and the violation of people's basic rights. It is the "JFDI" style of management—"Just flippin' do it."

It is this association with extreme negative role models that can sensitize the coach from straying into high challenge/low support. However, oversensitivity to this quadrant may cause the final, high challenge/high support quadrant also to be avoided, and this denies challenge its appropriate and helpful role in the coaching relationship. High challenge/low support interventions are characterized by being direct, blunt, aggressive, judgmental, unexpected, personal, emotionally charged, risky, and containing shock value. They make for amusing and entertaining viewing when used on "how to get on in business" television dramas, but in real life they don't produce sustainable levels of high performance in individuals or organizations.

The impact of high challenge/low support interventions between two people will be to create the conditions in which either the relationship ends prematurely or fear becomes the glue—the only thing that holds people together. Fear is a powerful agent of accountability and it does act as an effective motivator in crisis situations. For example, it is appropriate to be frightened of oncoming traffic and if that motivates you to get out of the way, that is effective behavior. The problem with fear as a sustainable tool of accountability is that fewer and fewer people are willing to put up with it in professional relationships. This is particularly true of the Generation Y workforce. These educated and empowered individuals will disengage either emotionally or physically, because they know that they have a choice and that losing their job is not the end of the world. They know this because it has happened to many of them before or to their friends and family. Generation Y is an interim generation not tied to any one organization or role.

While high challenge/low support interventions have earned themselves a bad name, we must nevertheless be careful as coaches that we don't "throw the baby out with the bathwater" by discounting the potential of challenging interventions to boost performance and growth. This brings us neatly to our final quadrant: high challenge, high support.

High challenge/high support

In the FACTS approach when working with accountability, we are aiming for the high challenge/high support quadrant of interventions and looking to work at accountability levels 1, 2, and 3: the person, the relationship/contract, and the organization as a whole. When faced with this CEO who has not done his homework, the FACTS coach could use any of the following interventions:

- ❑ "How would you react if one of your own direct reports did not complete the actions they had committed to?"
- ❑ "This is awkward. Part of me could let this go and part of me doesn't want to let you off the hook. What do you think?"
- ❑ "In our contract I said I would give you feedback and right now I am sat here wondering if you are really committed to this coaching work."
- ❑ "This is not what I expected and I am disappointed."
- ❑ "How would you explain this situation to one of your shareholders?"

The characteristics of these high challenge/high support interventions are:

- ❏ They are honest yet not judgmental.
- ❏ They take the conversation into the unknown.
- ❏ They are on the edge but are not directly confrontational.
- ❏ They often arise intuitively rather than being clever, pre-planned creations.
- ❏ They are often cheeky and humorous.
- ❏ They are risky yet motivated by genuine curiosity.

How these interventions are received will depend on the level of trust and respect that has been built into the relationship up to that point, together with the subtlety of tone and expression with which they are offered. They work best when effort has already been invested in the low challenge/high support quadrant. This creates the strong foundation that this riskier approach requires to be effective.

High challenge/high support interventions are an art as much as a science. The approach can be learned, but requires endless practice to achieve mastery, like a painter who may learn how to paint from reading a book, but learns so much more from the endless process of trial and error as canvas after canvas is experimented on. Unfortunately, there is no shortcut to achieving mastery. This type of intervention often goes hand in hand with Level 2 and Level 3 accountability. This is because the key to keeping the interventions neutral and impersonal is to bring in the perspective of other stakeholders and existing agreements. In the above examples, the perspective of the CEO's relationship to his own direct reports is used to generate challenge without judgment. In another, the value of the coaching contract to generate Level 2 accountability is demonstrated, since this can be referred to as a bilateral agreement that gives permission for the coach to make high challenge/high support interventions in the interest of achieving the goals of the work, not exerting power or ego.

In learning the art of high challenge/high support, one of the best guides is to recognize the unique impact of this coaching style when used alongside the strong base of high support/low challenge behaviors. In our experience, you know you have hit the high challenge/high support quadrant when you observe one or more of the following:

❏ Silence.
❏ A puzzled expression.
❏ Laughter.
❏ A sudden leap in tension.
❏ The presence of the ZOUD.
❏ A blank stare.
❏ Notable shifts in expression, energy, and body language.

A health warning: Situational coaching

We have tried to bring to life by practical examples the difference between normal accountability and FACTS accountability in coaching. Many coaches may already be working in this way and we hope that this kind of dialogue makes their natural, instinctive style more conscious to them and to others. Other coaches may see an opportunity to stretch their accountability skills through using the model and the levels outlined. Some may even recognize that the high challenge/high support quadrant is their natural habitat and that more work needs to be done in the high support/ low challenge quadrant of their coaching presence! However, in our experience, this latter group will be a minority. If a coach's default style is their only approach, then this will be limited in its effectiveness to certain types of people in certain situations—an unnecessary constraint.

Whenever a model is introduced, it is easy to get excited about it and believe that we have found *the* answer. We think that our life as a coach will suddenly get easier and we will be able to trot out our quadrants at every opportunity and use them to guide us in a reassuring, linear fashion. If nothing else, the FACTS approach is about engaging the real world and facing up to the truth. The truth of all models is that they are a gross simplification of reality and are dangerous in the hands of blind enthusiasts!

Even though we are passionate about this way of looking at the world and this way of talking about coaching interventions, we must issue a serious health warning: there is no right or wrong box of the support/challenge matrix to be in at any given time. We do believe that in an age of business renewal there is, on average, merit in reassessing your default position and questioning whether a shift to the high challenge/high support quadrant is appropriate. However, beyond this generic statement we acknowledge that depending on the individual, the coaching contract, the organizational culture, and a host of other factors, the coach must dynamically and instinctively choose the style of intervention that, on balance, best serves the situation.

For example, in an organization where the predominant management style is command and control, then regardless of whether we are in a boom period or a severe recession, a low challenge/high support style may be the best to adopt. This is because leaders in such an organization will be exposed to a high challenge/low support style every working hour and the coaching can have the most impact when aiming to balance this rather than exacerbate it.

Likewise, in a culture where relationships are prime and there is a cosiness of style that is jeopardizing bottom-line results, the most catalytic coaching interventions may be high challenge/ high support. Even bursts of high challenge/low support may be appropriate if the organization's very survival is in question, and a crisis response is perfectly justified when assessing Level 3 accountability.

The key for the experienced coach is to have access in the moment to the full range of possible responses. This requires confidence, flexibility, and a determination to work contrary to your natural style when it is in the service of the wider organization. This does not come naturally; it requires courage and conviction and a focus on a higher-level goal. It is like writing with your nondominant hand. At first this is awkward and clumsy, but over time you can build this capability if you have the determination to practice and persist.

It may help to think back to when you first encountered earlier coaching models such as GROW. Can you remember when these models and the emphasis on open questions and active listening felt unnatural and hard work? For the experienced coach or coaching leader these skills gradually become a new comfort zone. After a number of years building confidence and practicing new skills, the experienced coach uses them flexibly and intuitively.

In aiming for those dynamic choices about which quadrant of the box to work in with a particular client, the following factors are a useful guide:

❑ What is the level of trust in the relationship? The more trust that exists, the more risks can be taken that will not have a permanently damaging effect on the relationship if they go wrong. This allows experimental forays into high challenge/high support territory on a regular basis.

❑ What is the nature of the contract agreed? In particular, what outcomes are other stakeholders expecting and what did you and the coachee agree in terms of how accountability would operate in the relationship?

❏ What is your intuition? The world is far too complex and contains far too many unknown variables for even the cleverest of brains to be able to discern and process the necessary information in the time available. The only human characteristic that appears to work fast enough and accurately enough is the mysterious "right-brain" act of following your intuition. Trust it. Speak your truth!

❏ What is the level of tension in the room? We will explore this dynamic further when we consider the "T" in FACTS in Chapter 7, since the tension in the relationship is one important variable that the coach uses to calibrate their position on the support/challenge matrix.

❏ Finally, if in doubt, take the path that feels the hardest. When you are in the ZOUD and feeling the tension in the room, the chances are that you are getting close to a profound truth that could unlock great potential in the individual and the organization.

No one said it would be easy being a FACTS coach!

EXERCISE

Working in pairs or small groups, look back to the thought experiment introduced earlier in this chapter where you are asked to coach the CEO of a major financial institution just prior to the credit crunch of 2007–09. Think of a current challenge in your coaching or leadership role where the situation may have reached a similar critical tipping point and your intervention right now may have a profound impact. Once you have identified this scenario, focus in on the key individual or stakeholder with whom you need to have a conversation if you are to maximize the potential of the situation. Imagine your next conversation with this person and consider the four support/challenge quadrants in the diagram opposite.

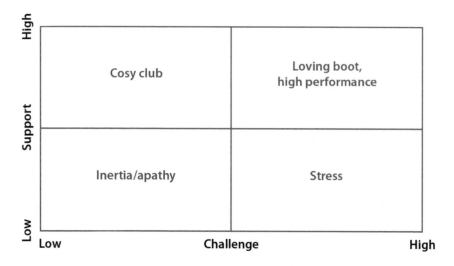

Take 10 minutes on your own to brainstorm at least five interventions that you could use in each quadrant that would focus on holding the individual accountable. Ensure that they reflect all three different levels of accountability in the FACTS approach: personal, relationship with you/coaching contract, and wider organization.

Once these are complete, take a further 15 minutes to ask your partner or peers in the group to validate and review these interventions and suggest alternative possibilities. Of the various interventions, identify the one that would be your normal approach in a situation like this. Finally, identify the intervention that would represent a stretch for you outside of your comfort zone and into the ZOUD. What would it take for you to choose and implement this stretch intervention?

FACTS example dialogue

You are working with Peter, the managing director of an international company, who has recently been appointed to his first role outside his home country. He is leading a large business services operation in Asia, based out of Singapore, and has requested help with adapting to some of the cross-cultural challenges in his role. You have contracted to carry out four telephone coaching sessions and a FACTS-based coaching agreement has been drawn up with Peter and his line manager in the UK.

In your first session, Peter established that one of his goals was to become more aware of his personal values so that he could use these to guide him in displaying consistent, confident behavior in a complex cross-cultural setting. As his coach, you carried out a simple values-elicitation exercise and it became clear that his #1 value was openness. It is now the second session and you are working on a more practical topic: the MD is planning a reorganization of his business and seeking your support about the best means of achieving this change efficiently and effectively.

In the session Peter starts to describe how he is planning to communicate the reorganization in different ways to different groups of staff, giving some more information than others and, in some cases, deliberately avoiding difficult questions to ensure that he does not upset vested interests. As a FACTS coach, what do you do next?

> COACH: Peter, I am feeling uncomfortable because in the first session you identified that openness was your number one value and now you are describing to me a communication approach that sounds closed and guarded.

[Coach working at Level 1 accountability.]
[Peter's eyes look to the window and he starts to think.]

> COACHEE: OK, you have a point. I am being closed and guarded in this session, but I am worried about the consequences of being open with everyone given this message.

COACH: Let's explore this some more. What is the worst that could happen if you are fully open with communicating the message regarding this reorganization to all parties?

COACHEE: I guess there could be some very difficult conversations, a lot of emotion, people threatening to resign, and a drop in morale that could damage performance.

COACH: And what is the best that could happen if you are fully open with communicating the message to all parties?

COACHEE: The best that could happen is that people understand the business need for me doing what I'm doing and respect the openness with which I am communicating. Despite some short-term concerns, in the medium term this should build a much stronger ethos and performance in the business.

COACH: What about other stakeholders in this situation? What are they expecting of you?

[Coach introduces Level 3 accountability.]

COACHEE: Well, my boss back in the UK is concerned that the changes need to be implemented sensitively, because in the past there have been all sorts of employee morale problems and attrition of key personnel due to a perceived "heavy-handed" style from people in my position.

COACH: Yes, I remember from my own conversations with him during the set-up of our coaching that this was a key issue. He mentioned he was worried that you didn't rush in "like a bull in a china shop," to use his words. What about your customers? What do they expect?

[Coach continues to explore Level 3 accountability.]

> COACHEE: Hmm, customers. Well, there is one customer here that accounts for 30 percent of our business and I know that the CEO of that organization has some very close personal relationships to members of my team who may be adversely affected by the changes I am proposing. In this part of the world, it is not a good idea to upset these personal relationships unless you have a very good reason to do so. The more I look at this, the more complex it seems to get!
>
> COACH: Yes, I agree. It is beginning to feel like we're going round in circles. I want to challenge you now to think of a creative way to move this situation forward, a way that allows you be authentic to your own values and also engage key stakeholders positively.

[Coach shares their own feelings, thus drawing on Level 2 accountability; that is, the personal relationship between coach and coachee.]

> COACHEE: OK, what I have realized is that the sequence of communication is important here. I can be open with all parties involved, but I need to think carefully about when I communicate the messages and to whom.
>
> COACH: Great, I think you are on to something. Tell me more.
>
> COACHEE: Well, I need to start with the CEO of our most important customer. A lunch with him to get to know

him better and to float some of my ideas and gauge
his reaction would be a sensible first step. Assuming
that this client CEO is on board, then I should talk to
my boss again and reassure him of the style in which
I will implement the changes: open, honest, yet sensitive. Only then should I move to the communication
plans for all staff.

COACH: What if your client CEO doesn't buy into the
changes and regards them as unwise?

[Coach returns to Level 3 accountability to explore the customer
perspective more fully.]

COACHEE: It depends on his strength of opinion, but if
this is the case then I can't risk this relationship and
I would need to go back to my boss and be open and
honest with him that I do not think these changes are
appropriate right now and that I've changed my mind
about the best way forward in the short term.

COACH: That would certainly be a different but equally
valid way of honoring your value of openness and
honesty. What is left for us to do on this topic?

COACHEE: Nothing. I am clear about the way forward and
I will ask my PA to set up the lunch with the client
CEO immediately after our session. It seems an obvious step now that I've had the chance to take a step
back and explore the situation from a number of different perspectives.

CHAPTER 6

FACTS—Courageous goals

The world we live in requires great courage and patience.
(Tao Te Ching, Verse 73)

The "C" in FACTS represents courageous goals. Like feedback and accountability, goal setting is a standard component of traditional coaching approaches. It is featured in all the major coaching texts, training courses, and the competency frameworks of the professional bodies. So what is new about goal setting in the FACTS approach?

In this chapter we propose that existing goal-setting models such as SMART and PRISM are rational, left-brain approaches that lack an emotional heart; specifically, they lack courage as a component of transformative goal setting. We suggest that transformative goal setting is appropriate in an age of business renewal when an incremental, linear path may no longer serve leadership needs. We describe an alternative goal-setting approach and explore this in the context of executive coaching and a coaching style of leadership. We also feature the work of Joseph Campbell and his "hero's journey" as a road map for the process involved in achieving courageous goals. Finally, we link this back to our cornerstone of the support/challenge matrix and explore the impact of courageous goals against this dynamic.

Traditional goal setting

SMART goal setting was a phrase first coined in the 1960s, although its exact origins are hard to trace. It has gradually crept into the mainstream of management thinking and is now applied routinely around the globe. While there are many variations of the acronym SMART, our own preferred interpretation is:

> S: specific
> M: measurable
> A: agreed
> R: realistic
> T: timelined

In SMART goal setting, all goal descriptions are validated against these criteria as a means of refining the goal and giving its expression as much impact as possible. For example, the vague aspiration "My goal is to increase sales" when validated using the SMART criteria might become "My goal is to increase sales of widgets by 25 percent in the next six months." No one can argue with the practical success of this model and its ease of use among leaders and coaches. It is a model that we intuitively use ourselves in all our assignments as part of agreeing coaching assignments and measuring success.

A similar but less well-known goal-setting model is PRISM:

> P: personal
> R: realistic
> I: interesting
> S: specific
> M: measurable

PRISM shares many characteristics with the SMART approach, but adds "personal" and "interesting" as means of making sure that the individual is motivated toward the achievement of the goals as well as accepting their rational validity. A SMART goal may be rejected because it is simply too boring and irrelevant to the personal drivers of the individual who owns it. For example, an extrovert individual who thrives on networking may struggle to be motivated by the SMART goal "Write a book on my own over the next nine months."

While both SMART and PRISM serve a purpose, we do not believe that they are models that tap into the full potential of individuals, teams, and organizations. They draw too heavily on the resources of the left brain and too little on those of the right brain. Specifically, they are intellectually sound approaches that follow a structured, linear path, yet they fail to engage the components of heart and spirit that are often characteristic of our most profound achievements. They tick the box marked IQ but do not tick the boxes marked EQ (emotional intelligence) and SQ (spiritual intelligence). In practice, this left-brain bias of traditional goal setting is likely to generate incremental goals that are risk averse and safe, as opposed to transformative goals that are bold and exciting.

Do we need transformational goals in order to plot a course out of the challenges we currently face, or do we need more of the same, incremental goals that build on pre-existing paradigms and ways of doing business? This is not a trivial debate, yet in some areas it would appear that our current approaches are approaching their natural limits. As the world of business becomes more complex, more global, and increasingly subject to external pressures ranging from climate change to regulation to technological innovation, can incremental goal-setting models like PRISM and SMART meet the needs of today's business leaders and their coaches?

Courageous goal setting

The alternative is to seek a goal-setting approach that taps into the potential of the right brain and use this alongside the existing models. Such an approach would generate goals that have the following characteristics:

- ❏ Excitement
- ❏ Fear
- ❏ Inspiration
- ❏ Imagination
- ❏ Wonder
- ❏ Adventure

Immediately, you will sense a "buzz" about these words that was lacking from the SMART and PRISM examples. Any goal that has these characteristics will require one attribute above all: courage! Without courage such right-brain goals will quickly be dismissed as too difficult, too risky, and too painful. Courage is an attribute that runs throughout the FACTS approach, since it requires courage to challenge someone, whether through holding them accountable, giving feedback, or holding tension. But the process of coaching starts with goal setting. If the goals themselves are not courageous then this will limit all the subsequent steps.

The table overleaf contrasts a series of SMART goals with their courageous equivalents to give a further example of the difference between the two. As you read these, take a moment to gauge the impact of the words in each statement and assess their difference in terms of their potential to motivate and inspire.

The last example in the table highlights most vividly the difference between coaching others to reach incremental, developmental goals and coaching them to achieve radical, transformative goals. In explaining to people the difference between teaching and coaching we are often reminded of the question: "Can you teach a caterpillar to fly?" You can't, but you can help unlock its natural potential to transform into a butterfly by creating the environment in which this is most likely to occur. Do any of us really understand what happens in that dark cocoon? For most of us it is beyond intellectual explanation, but it does happen day after day, year after year. If this is the potential of a humble caterpillars then what might be the potential of a human being?

SMART goal	Courageous goal
In the next year we will see advances in science that will allow us to send a manned spacecraft into orbit round the Earth.	In the next decade we will land a man on the moon.
As a team we will increase our sales by 10% in the next quarter.	As a team we will close the largest deal we have ever made in the next quarter.
My goal as CEO of this company is to increase the share price by 20% over a three-year period.	My goal as CEO of this company is to eliminate the disease malaria from the world by 2015.
My goal is to be promoted to the next level of this organization within three years.	My goal is to be the first female director of marketing of this company by the time I am 35.
My goal is to write an article for the local newspaper in the next three months.	My goal is to write a global bestselling book that is translated into 11 different languages by 2013.
This team will cut costs in this company by 20% in the next year.	Over the next year, this team will lead a radical reorganization of this company while raising employee engagement scores across all functions.
I want to be a bigger, faster caterpillar.	I want to be a butterfly.

The world of nature gives us another example of transformative change that is much closer to home for most of us: adolescence. Anyone who has lived with a teenager will have witnessed the miraculous process of transformative change. At times they may have thought that the teenager disappeared into their own cocoon, sealed away from the outside world and permanently plugged into their iPod. They may have also observed them confused and in a dark place and been tempted to poke around in their being with the best of intentions, yet betraying an underlying lack of trust in the natural process of change. A parent through this stage is also a FACTS coach, balancing support and challenge and hoping that the trust built in the teenager's formative years is sufficient to sustain the turmoil of adolescent change.

In 1994 Jim Collins and Jerry Porras wrote *Built to Last*. The book covered a broad range of factors contributing to organizational success over a long period, and they also coined the term BHAG for "big, hairy, audacious goal." According to Collins and Porras, "a true BHAG is clear and compelling, serves as a unifying focal point of effort. It is tangible, energizing, people get it straight away... it takes little or no explanation." For them BHAGs were more than objectives that companies hoped to accomplish over the coming days, months, or years; they were outrageous, visionary, game-changing goals that defined a whole epoch of a company's existence. This is the essence of what we refer to as courageous goals.

In an organizational context, Collins and Porras quoted goals such as:

- ❏ Wal-Mart (1990): To become a $125 billion company by the year 2000.
- ❏ Boeing (1950): To become the dominant player in commercial aircraft and bring the world into the jet age.

❑ Philip Morris (1950): To dislodge RJ Reynolds as the number one tobacco company in the world.
❑ Nike (1960): To crush Adidas!

At their core, these courageous goals have the following characteristics:

❑ They are outrageous—the first reaction to a courageous goal should be: "That's impossible!"
❑ They are frightening—the second reaction should be: "Even if it were possible, it would frighten the life out of me to commit to it!"
❑ They are transformative—the third reaction should be: "If we did this then my whole world and our whole organization will have changed in a way that I cannot fully imagine right now."

Lessons from Olympic sport

In the world of sport, there are many examples of courageous goals at a personal and team level that form the basis of truly inspirational achievements. One that we are particularly close to is the story of Alan Campbell, the UK single scull rower, and his coach Bill Barry, with whom we worked as part of the leadership transformation consultancy 121partners.

Bill, an Olympic medalist himself, first met Alan in 2003 when he watched him rowing at their local Tideway Scullers club in London. From a distance, Bill observed a gawky, overweight, novice rower whose technique was uncoordinated and clumsy. When Alan emerged from the boat that day, Bill asked him what his goal was. Alan replied, "I want to win the Olympic gold medal in the single scull in Beijing in 2008." This was a truly outrageous statement for which there was no evidence or credibility. However, when Bill looked into Alan's eyes he recognized a steely determination and a heart of courage that somehow made him hesitate before dismissing the youngster's ambition. Clearly, if Alan did win the goal medal in Beijing it would transform his world out of all recognition, hence here was an example of a well-crafted goal: outrageous, courageous, and transformative.

That day Bill took Alan at his word and formed a coaching partnership that over the next seven years took in the following milestones:

☐ 2004: Alan participates in the Athens Olympics in the GB eight boat.
☐ 2005: Alan wins the GB single scull final.
☐ 2006: Alan wins his first world cup regatta in Munich, beating the existing world champion.
☐ 2007: Alan comes fourth in the world championships in the UK.
☐ 2008: Alan suffers a knee injury eight weeks before the Beijing Olympics, is ruled out of participation by medical experts, yet recovers to take fifth place in the Olympic final, 4.64 seconds behind the winner
☐ 2009: Alan breaks the world record and gains silver medal in the world championships in Poland.
☐ 2010: Alan wins bronze medal in the world championships held in New Zealand and remains in clear contention for the Olympic gold medal in London in 2012.

Bill and Alan have a unique partnership as coach and athlete. Their story is an inspiring example of a coach's total belief in an athlete's potential acting as an empowering challenge to pursue the dream goal. We can compare this story with the world of business. Would you secretly laugh at your coachee if they declared their own courageous goal as Alan did to Bill back in 2003, or would you take them at their word and commit to a partnership that leads you, them, and their organization to the heady heights of world-class achievements? What is it about the world of business that gets in the way of the declaration of courageous goals and restricts commitment to such bold endeavors? Maybe we are too evaluative, too critical, and too risk averse.

Bill and Alan often speak to audiences of business leaders to share the lessons from working together as coach and athlete. They present their business plan, which looks like this:

A simple, straight line of continuous improvement. There is no sophistication in this message: it is a story of determination and the power of the human will rather than complexity and the power of the human intellect. It is a right-brain business plan that does not worry about the "how," but simply states the "what" and requires the total commitment of coach and coachee.

Bill and Alan also have a mission statement, a poem by Guillaume Apollinaire called "Come to the Edge":

"Come to the edge."
"We can't. We're afraid."
"Come to the edge."
"We can't. We will fall!"
"Come to the edge."
And they came.
And he pushed them.
And they flew.

Are you willing to come to the edge as a coach and to work at the edge with your business "athletes" to achieve courageous goals? Do you really believe in the miraculous potential of the average human being?

In the world of sport there appears to be a culture conducive to setting and pursuing courageous goals that is rarely experienced in the world of business. In our experience of working with both athletes and business leaders, we have observed the following cultural differences that contribute to this divide:

❑ *Fear of failure*—athletes embrace failure as an inevitable fact of life and its occurrence does not crush their self-esteem but drives them onward. In business, failure seems to carry a stigma of shame that undermines the confidence of a leader and their team to a much greater degree. Hence the risk of failure is reduced by avoiding commitment and responsibility and diluting the ambitiousness of goals.

❑ *Lack of alignment of goals between organization, team, leader, and individual*—in sport the finishing line is clear and unambiguous for all the stakeholders involved. In business this is not true: the difference between winning and losing is often subjective and open to the vagaries of political interpretation. What aggravates this is a lack of focus on the alignment of goals between stakeholders at the outset of a plan and the regular recontracting of goals as the plan is implemented.

❑ *The inhibiting link of goals to remuneration, promotion, and bonus schemes*—most goal setting in business occurs in the context of an annual appraisal process that also governs the payment of rewards and promotion decisions. This reality inhibits individuals from aiming as high as they might, since they fear the impact of missing their targets on their compensation package. To avoid this, courageous goal setting needs to be an additional, independent conversation rather than an adjunct to the existing performance review process.

❑ *Unnecessary complexity*—as Bill and Alan's business plan demonstrates, the world of sport is often direct, simple, and transparent. Business plans run to many pages, many spreadsheets, and many appendices. A focus on intellectual analysis rather than courageous dreaming squeezes the excitement and motivation out of the goal-setting process.

Dream, share, start

Where does the coach fit into this picture? We believe there is a unique opportunity for coaches to overlay business-as-usual SMART goal setting with an additional, extra conversation around courageous goals. Unconnected to corporate performance management processes, courageous goal setting becomes a liberating personal conversation. Divorced from promotion panels and bonus thresholds, the courageous goals mindset allows people to have a dream for the sake of having a dream. It frees up the leader, the coach, and the team to build beyond the limited framework of traditional performance management systems and stretch into the exciting, scary world of the impossible.

If this is a prospect that appeals to you, then how do you help others create and commit to courageous goals? Here is a simple three-step structure that will kick-start the conversation with individuals or teams.

Step 1: Dream!
In this step, the coach gives permission for the coachee to dream. They challenge the coachee to forget about the constraints of the present moment and the perceived difficulties in achieving the

goal and simply to focus on the dream. Questions that support this step might be:

- ❑ "What would be your equivalent of winning an Olympic gold medal?"
- ❑ "If you believed that anything was possible, what would you want to achieve?"
- ❑ "If there were no constraints around you, what is the limit of your potential?"
- ❑ "If you believed in yourself 110 percent, what would you be capable of achieving?"
- ❑ "How far into the future would we need to set this goal in order for you to let go of worrying how it might be achieved?"
- ❑ "What if you were being even bolder in your thinking?"
- ❑ "What if you had all the support you needed, what would be possible then?"

These questions unshackle the coachee's imagination and prompt them to declare what really lies in their heart. The mere act of declaring such well-protected secrets is often itself a hugely liberating experience for the coachee.

The coach can then move to validate that this goal meets the criteria of a courageous undertaking. This test rests on the coachee's emotional reaction to the goal rather than their intellectual assessment. The challenge for the coach is to keep the coachee's left brain shackled and to continue to let the right brain lead and express itself fully. Questions that help in this stage include:

- ❑ "How do you feel about this goal?"
- ❑ "What level of excitement does this goal conjure up for you?"
- ❑ "What level of fear does this goal evoke in you?"

- ❑ "For what reason is this a game-changing goal?"
- ❑ "When have you felt this way about a goal before?"
- ❑ "What inspires you most about this goal?"
- ❑ "What is still left unsaid?"

Step 2: Share!

Once a courageous goal has been declared to the coach and validated, the coach challenges the coachee to find an opportunity to share the goal publicly outside of the confidential coaching conversation.

Questions that would prompt this step include:

- ❑ "Who do you trust sufficiently to share this goal with?"
- ❑ "Who could help you if you shared this goal with them?"
- ❑ "If you were feeling at your most courageous, who else would you be sharing this goal with?"

The value of sharing courageous goals links back to the "A" in FACTS, accountability. A goal shared publicly brings with it a degree of accountability that commits the coachee to their path. It is also linked to the "F" in FACTS, feedback. When they share the goal the coachee will receive valuable feedback. This feedback can be brought to the next coaching conversation for discussion and reflection.

Step 3: Start!

The coachee does not need to know how this courageous goal will become a reality, but they do need to take the first step. As the Chinese philosopher Lao Tzu noted, "A journey of a thousand miles begins with a single step." The first step is the point of commitment, when the world knows you are serious. In the words of German philosopher Goethe:

Until one is committed, there is hesitancy, the chance to draw back, always ineffectiveness. Concerning all acts of initiative (and creation), there is one elementary truth the ignorance of which kills countless ideas and splendid plans: that the moment one definitely commits oneself, then providence moves too. All sorts of things occur to help one that would never otherwise have occurred. A whole stream of events issues from the decision, raising in one's favor all manner of unforeseen incidents and meetings and material assistance, which no man could have dreamed would have come his way. Whatever you can do or dream you can, begin it. Boldness has genius, power and magic in it. Begin it now.

In Step 3, the coach challenges the coachee to identify and commit to the first step in moving toward the courageous goal. It is important to stress that there is no order of magnitude involved in taking the first step; in other words, the first step can be very, very small, but this does not reduce its potential as a means of mobilizing the coachee on their journey. If the step requires courage to take, this is the sole criterion against which its value is assessed. For this reason the first step may sound trivial or silly to the outside observer. It is important that the coach does not stray into judgment and risk killing off the first, fragile movements toward the end goal.

Questions that can help in this phase include:

❑ "What is the smallest tangible step you could make toward this goal in the next week?"
❑ "What next step could you take that would send yourself a signal that you are serious about this goal?"
❑ "What is the next step you could take that would be really exciting?"

❑ "What is a step you could take next that means a lot to you even if others may consider it to be trivial?"

❑ "What support would you value from me in taking this next step?"

❑ "Who else can help you take this step successfully?"

This three-step model mobilizes the will and engages the coachee's vision. Most of all, it stirs up the coachee's courage and creates a spirit of adventure that is often lacking from the daily chores of business life. The coach is there to facilitate this process: to challenge, to support, and to use the FACTS coaching principles and approach to ensure that business as usual doesn't prevail.

Revisiting the support/challenge matrix

What is the impact of a courageous goal on the support/challenge matrix? It is our view that the courageous goal defines the scale of the matrix itself. This is best represented in a diagram:

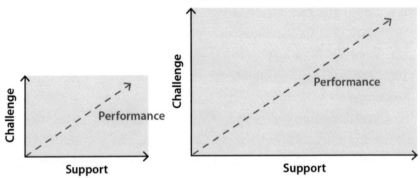

The courageous goal stretches the axes of both the support and the challenge aspects of the matrix. The courageous goal demands an order of magnitude difference in both the level of support and the level of challenge that the coach needs to bring to the coaching relationship. Both extend in equal measure in order to create a transformational space rather than a developmental space.

This impact has significant implications for the contracting conversation that precedes any commitment of coach and coachee to this style of engagement. Are both parties willing to take a risk, to commit to this endeavor, to build the mutual trust and respect that it requires, and to contemplate the very real joy and pain that any such ambition involves? This is not a trivial undertaking. The principle of building the contract and honoring the contract assumes a new significance in the context of a courageous goal. Both parties look into each other's eyes and ask: "Are you up for this?" As each success and failure comes along, the question is asked again: "Are you still up for this? Are you prepared to come to the edge, to be pushed, and to fly?"

Parallels with the hero's journey

When we present the information in this chapter we often get feedback from seminar participants that it reminds them of the work of Joseph Campbell, who coined the phrase the "hero's journey" to describe great mythological stories over time and across cultures. He observed that in these stories there were a number of common steps, which he chronicled in *The Hero with a Thousand Faces*. These steps can be observed in many heroic tales, such as *Star Wars*, the Harry Potter series, and *The Lord of the Rings*. In essence, the hero's journey charts the process for achieving courageous goals. Let's briefly review the three stages he observed in this context:

❑ *Departure*—the budding hero leaves the familiar world behind, heeding the call and crossing the first threshold into the field of adventure.

❑ *Initiation*—the budding hero learns to navigate the unfamiliar world of adventure with its series of tests, encounters with friends and foes, and discovery of hidden treasures.

❑ *Return*—the proven hero returns to the familiar world with their discovered treasure together with the wisdom of the journey, which can now be shared with others.

These overall phases and their more detailed steps are shown in the diagram below:

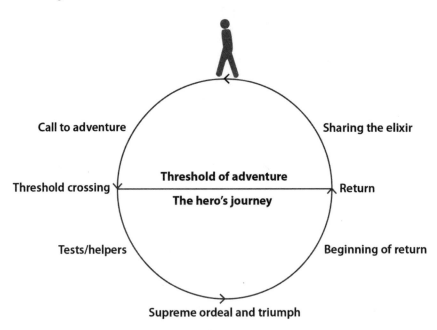

Why would the world of business and business leadership not be an arena of adventure for the budding hero and heroine? Armed with abundant will and a courageous goal, why would you not set out on this exciting journey that is so far removed from the drudgery of SMART goals, annual performance appraisals, and salary increments? As the diagram indicates, it is a cycle of courageous goals that can be repeated over a career. To avoid stagnation, new goals are set, new thresholds are crossed, and new treasures discovered. The hero's journey never really ends.

In such a journey, 90 percent of the focus is on our hero or heroine because it is their storyline that is being written. However, in the small print of the journey we observe the unique role of what Campbell refers to as helpers, who appear at different stages in the journey to guide the hero to their ultimate goal. Are these helpers not really coaches who can be engaged in the pursuit of transformational goals? The hero needs helpers to speed them on the quest; they are adding something that the hero cannot do on their own.

The helper may be a hero in their own right, someone who has had their own hero's journey and is now taking part in that of the new hero-to-be. In modern mythology these are characters like Trinity in *The Matrix*, Legolas in *The Lord of the Rings,* or Sallah in *Indiana Jones and the Last Crusade.* The helper is often symbolized as an old man or woman, their age representing the wisdom that they offer generously. A common feature of the helper that chimes with the coaching role is that at some point they step aside and let the hero be a hero; they challenge the hero to evidence their own courage and resist the temptation to rescue them or fear for their failure. These coaches are brave enough to let go of the hero and they are secure enough in their own identity that they don't any longer need to play the hero role for themselves. This is the true test of the strength and maturity of the FACTS coach.

The courageous goal is fundamental to the support/challenge matrix because it defines the order of magnitude of both the support and the challenge that will be necessary for those who are helpers to business heroes in the making. We are left with the overriding question of whether the business paradigm is truly a transformative arena as opposed to an incremental one. For sure, an age of business renewal will challenge this notion further. Will the global challenges of climate change, poverty, natural resource exploitation, and population explosion drive the need for transformative solutions, transformative leaders, and transformative coaches in the years to come?

EXERCISE

This is a timeline exercise that helps the hero as they encounter trials, which are an inevitable part of any adventure. The coach acts a guide to lead the coachee through the following steps.

In a spacious room with the coach and the "hero" standing together, the coach asks the coachee to decide where on the floor the present and the future are located. The future position should correspond to the state when the courageous goal has been fully achieved. The coach asks the coachee if these places, representing the present and the future, are joined, and if so, how. Once the coachee explains, neither coach nor client steps into or crosses the space that connects the present with the future. The coach asks the coachee to step into the spot identified as the future when the courageous goal has been fully achieved.

The coach asks the coachee to get to know this space and to describe it. "What does it feel like?" "What can they see?" "What thoughts do you have in this place?" "Who is with you in this place?" As the coachee talks, the coach asks questions to help the coachee clarify their thoughts and feelings. The coach makes notes of what is said. The coach encourages the coachee to talk in the present tense, saying "What I'm feeling here is..." rather than "What I would be feeling here might be..." The coach then asks: "When you look back at a younger you who is looking at the path, what advice would you give to your younger self?" As the coachee talks, the coach asks questions to help clarify their thinking and notes what they say.

The coach then instructs the coachee: "What I'd like you to do now is to walk back along the timeline to the present and identify the key steps from the present state to where you are now." As the coachee walks back along the timeline and talks, the coach makes notes while inviting the coachee to share through open questions such as "Where did you become discouraged?" "How did you gain fresh motivation?" "Who helped you?" "What were the defining moments?" "What was important about taking this particular step?" The coach encourages the coachee to use the past tense in their answers.

Once the coachee reaches the place designated as the present, the coach asks them to step off the timeline and contemplate it from a distance. When they have done this, the coach asks: "What can you learn from this more objective perspective?"

The coach now asks the coachee to step back into the position in the room that represents the future and asks: "What does your younger self back there in the present moment need to hear from you?" Now the coach requests the coachee to step off the timeline completely. With the coachee looking at the timeline, the coach says: "In one minute I'm going to ask you to step into the place representing the present and collect the information or learning in whatever way you like so that it becomes yours." After a period of reflection, the coachee steps back into the space that represents the present moment. The coach congratulates them on completing their hero's journey and the two conduct a debrief on the experience, generating any immediate actions that the coachee feels compelled to take.

FACTS example dialogue

You have been working with Georgia, a senior program manager at an international company, for 12 months. The first phase of coaching has been completed and the goals achieved to the satisfaction of Georgia and her sponsoring line manager. Initially Georgia was in a difficult place, having received negative feedback from some key sponsors. However, she has worked hard to change perceptions of her behavior in key areas and has built a new base of confidence and respect with her peers. You are now starting a second phase of coaching and are recontracting with Georgia and her new line manager for a further series of coaching sessions. You are conscious that you have built a solid base of mutual trust and respect with Georgia and need to push on to leverage this relationship and ensure that the second wave of coaching has as much impact as the first. As a FACTS coach you are keen to avoid any risk of complacency or "business as usual" creeping into the relationship.

In the first session of this second wave, you have reviewed the success of the first coaching sessions and established lessons learned, and are now turning to setting new goals for the next phase of the work.

> COACH: So, Georgia, what are your goals for this next phase of coaching?
>
> COACHEE: I want to achieve my full potential in the company.

[Vague, ill-defined goal.]

> COACH: OK, tell me a bit more about that.
>
> COACHEE: Well, there is a company-wide problem with customer service that has been highlighted from recent client feedback.
>
> COACH: What is the link between achieving your full potential and the customer service challenge?
>
> COACHEE: I figure that if I could have a positive impact on an issue of that magnitude then I would have achieved my full potential. For example, I know the director,

Brian, who is responsible for customer service and I have offered Brian my support and that of my peers to help improve customer service through a specific initiative.

COACH: What would be the measure of success for this goal?

[Coach uses the SMART model to make the goal more specific and measurable.]

COACHEE: The client survey will be repeated at the end of this year and the company is aiming for a 30 percent improvement.

COACH: How about your own personal measure of success for reaching your full potential in this area?

[Coach uses the PRISM model to request a more personal definition of success.]

COACHEE: I want to help and support Brian, but I don't need this to be recognized by either money or status.

COACH: You don't need money or status recognition. What sort of recognition do you need?

COACHEE: I'll just know that I made a difference and I'll feel good about that.

COACH: This is beginning to sound vague to me. I'm imagining meeting with you at the end of the year and you telling me that you achieved your goal and you feel good about it, but what would be the proof of that?

[Coach challenges coachee for the first time.]

COACHEE: Other people would believe it to be true as well.
COACH: And how would that be measured?

[Coach challenges coachee for the second time.]

COACHEE: There is an annual award for customer service that my peers would vote for. However, I don't want to set this as a measure of success, because it is out of my control and I would be very disappointed if I set this as a measure and then failed to achieve it.
COACH: Hmm, sounds a fantastic measure of success to me.

[Coach challenges coachee for the third time]

COACHEE: But it's really not important to me to win the award.
COACH: Is that true?

[Coach challenges coachee for the fourth time]

COACHEE: I think so.
COACH: How would you feel if you did set this as a measure of success and you achieved it?

[Coach introduces a courageous goal and asks the coachee to assess this emotionally, not intellectually.]

COACHEE: It would be a great feeling. I would be absolutely thrilled!
COACH: Let me play devil's advocate here. How do you know that you're not shying away from this goal because you're frightened of failing to achieve it?

[Coach sticks with the emotional assessment and accuses the coachee of not being brave enough to take on the goal. The tension in the conversation is rising and rapport is being stretched by the challenging style of the interventions.]

> COACHEE: Well, you know me pretty well now. We've worked together for 12 months. What do you think?

[Coachee takes the challenge on the chin and requests an honest opinion from the coach.]

> COACH: I think there's a risk that you're playing safe. A year ago you were establishing yourself in the role, but you've done that now. I've seen you make great progress and I think you can now stretch for a more exciting and courageous goal.

[Coach speaks their truth and encourages the coachee through their genuine belief in their full potential.]

> COACHEE: I need to take this away and think about it some more.
> COACH: That's fine. This would be a big step and a significant commitment. I want you to know that if you're up for that goal then I'm up for helping you.

[Coach makes the decision to back off from the challenge and to switch to offering support on the assumption that the coachee commits to the courageous goal.]

> COACHEE: Thanks. If I take this on I'm certainly going to need some help.

COACH: Let's start as we mean to go on. How can I help with the next step?

COACHEE: Just keep challenging me. I'll tell you if it gets too much. Call me in a week's time and ask me where I've got to with crafting the goal and measure of success.

COACH: OK, I'll do that. Let's speak then.

CHAPTER 7
FACTS—Tension

*A raging wind cannot blow all morning nor a sudden rain-
storm last throughout the day. (Tao Te Ching, Verse 23)*

More than ever, maximizing individual performance is crucial: everyone is required to do more and dig deeper.
Coaching has an important role to play in pushing performance
and stretching the boundaries of personal capability. Each person
has a unique optimal level of tension. What is the impact of this
for the coach and coachee interacting and how do we calibrate the
tension within our laboratory of learning, our coaching room? In
this chapter we focus on how to create constructive tension once
courageous goals have been set, feedback delivered, and accountability held.

Optimal levels of tension: The Yerkes–Dodson law

Tension is an unusual word in relation to coaching; we don't nor-
mally expect our coaching sessions to be tense. Typically tension
is considered a bad thing and something to be avoided. Tension
leads to stress, and hypertension is a chronic medical condition.
Health advisers ask us to actively reduce stress and relax. Studies
have shown that the US workforce is experiencing increasing levels of stress as a result of demands such as broadening job scope,
greater workloads, and job uncertainty. This increase in stress has
a direct impact on reducing employee satisfaction, commitment,
and retention. Some firms have been taken to court by employees
who have felt overwhelmed by stress caused by their employer.

To counter the impact of stress, many organizations have implemented stress-awareness training so that managers can spot the signs and take steps to reduce stress for their employees. We fully agree that stress is debilitating and unhealthy both mentally and physically; it should be avoided and measures adopted to reduce it if it does occur. But the business world can tend to be ultra-cautious and risk averse, avoiding even the slightest hint of tension. It is as if the word "tension" is interchangeable with "stress." This is allowing the pendulum to swing too far in the opposite direction, leading to a polarized reaction where tension is avoided in every situation. We believe that in fact appropriate tension can produce positive results that are valuable for individuals and the organizations they work for.

Anecdotally, we can all think of stressful situations that were overwhelming and negatively affected our performance. Remember the first time you had to deliver a presentation or a speech, for example. But can you also think of a situation when you were relaxed and so laid back that you weren't "up for the job" and you didn't perform as well as you could have done? In contrast, can you remember a worrying situation in which anxiety produced a level of tension that upped your game and led to you surprising yourself at the level of performance you were able to achieve? So tension can help to increase performance, but too much tension can lead to stress and reduced performance.

There has been a great deal of research in this area, particularly by Scandinavian psychologists in the 1970s and 1980s. For example, Finnish high school students undertaking an important six-hour exam showed that adrenalin increases were correlated to improved exam performance. Further back, in 1908, American psychologists Robert M. Yerkes and John Dillingham Dodson identified a link between performance and arousal, in that performance increased up to a point and then began to decrease.

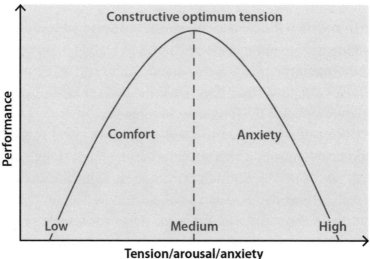

They used mice in their laboratory work, but this performance/ arousal link has since been replicated by many other psychologists and with human subjects. This is a psychological principle that has lasted the test of time and the relationship is known as the Yerkes–Dodson law, represented in the diagram above.

The Yerkes–Dodson law dictates that performance increases with physiological or mental arousal up to an optimal level; when the arousal level passes this optimal point performance decreases. There are three sections to the performance–tension curve. The left-hand section of the inverted "U" is where tension is low and performance is also low. This can be a boring place and some people have called it the "rustout" zone. Someone working on a task in this zone is likely to be easily distracted on the lookout for more stimulating activities. They are unlikely to be motivated, as the activity they are involved in, or task they are undertaking, is just too dull. The far-right section of the curve is caused by the negative effects of stress, with too much tension and over-arousal. Burnout occurs and performance drops off considerably. It is characterized by a sense of being overwhelmed physically and mentally: there is too much work to do in too little time, or the task is too complex, and the situation is hopeless. Physically the heart rate can increase, breathing may become faster and shallower, and long-term stress can have other physical effects harmful to health. When stressed, a person is likely to disengage from the task, be demotivated, be distracted, and over the long term become ill.

The middle section of the Yerkes–Dodson curve is the peak performance zone, in which tension is at an optimal level and individuals and teams display high performance, high motivation, high energy, high engagement, and psychological wellbeing. This is the golden zone: the optimal area for each person or team to recognize for themselves and strive toward in order to achieve peak performance and wellbeing. For leaders, this is the area in which their team members will perform their best work, be most innovative, and create the most value for the organization. The leader's role is to create the conditions to optimize tension across the organization so that each person achieves peak performance. In sporting terms it has been described as "being in the zone" or "in the flow."

The Yerkes–Dodson law has been replicated many times, so we accept that it is true and that tension is not necessarily bad; it can be a force for good and not something that should be avoided at all costs. Think of tension as potential energy and imagine a rubber band that is stretched: as the tension of the band increases, it holds more energy. Think about a child flicking a rubber band by holding one end over the thumb of his left hand and stretching the other end with the thumb and forefinger of his right hand. The more the child stretches the band, the more tension there is. When the child lets go, the band flies through the air. With more stretch there is more energy, so the band will travel further. If there is not enough energy, the band will flop to the floor. However, if the child stretches and stretches the band and does not release it, eventually the tension becomes too great and the band snaps.

To apply the Yerkes–Dodson law we must be able to recognize the benefits of optimum levels of tension, to recognize that this will contribute to achieving a peak performance level, but be sensitive to the signs of stress and suboptimal performance. The assumption here is that tension is a dynamic force and, as with our rubber band example, it can be increased and decreased. Individuals and coaches can actively manage the levels of tension, which is done through awareness and interventions designed to increase, decrease, or maintain an optimal level.

Linking the Yerkes–Dodson law to our support/challenge matrix, we would say that the left-hand side of the performance curve is the "cosy club" and the right-hand side is where challenge is high and support is low, with stress evident. The middle section of the curve is in the high performance, "loving boot" quadrant of the support/challenge matrix. The central area of the curve is the space for growth and development, the fertile ground for coaching. It is interesting to superimpose the two diagrams to explain this connection.

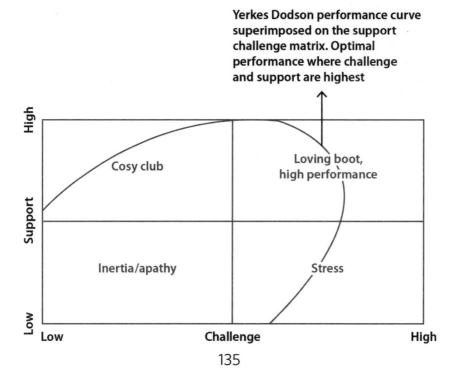

Yerkes Dodson performance curve superimposed on the support challenge matrix. Optimal performance where challenge and support are highest

Calibrating the coachee's tension

What are the implications for coaching and development? Because of the strong link coaching has with the "sister" profession of counseling, some coaches believe that coaching should be supportive and not challenging. However, the big difference between counseling and coaching is not what the practitioners do; it's who they're working with. Typically, people who go to see counsellors are saying: "I'm not functioning properly and I want to be fixed and feel better." Someone seeing a counselor is likely to have high levels of tension or anxiety and may already be in the suboptimal area of performance. If this is the case, the counselor will consciously create the conditions to reduce tension and anxiety and hold a very relaxed session to bring the client to the optimal level of arousal. The amount of tension a person in this state can withstand is much lower than for the average senior executive in a major company who is functioning well and not in need of therapeutic input. In business and the world of coaching, coachees are typically high-performing, high-achieving, high-potential individuals who are intact and resourceful; many actually thrive on tension.

So as executive coaches it is our duty to work constructively and use tension as a tool when we interact with highly effective people who are striving for courageous goals. How do we know what the right level of tension is? Each coachee will have a natural starting point for arousal that will indicate the position of the optimal level of tension. The coach is in the laboratory of learning, undertaking observations to create the conditions that produce that level. Each coaching intervention, question, or activity will produce different levels of tension for each person. The coach can "calibrate" the coachee's responses to determine the interventions that are too relaxed (in the cosy club) and not sufficiently tense, and conversely to understand when the tension is too high, performance dips, and stress occurs. This calibration is done by observing the coachee, their body language, tone of voice, eye contact, the number and length of pauses in their speech, and what is said. The coach can observe a baseline of these behaviors and get a feel for the typical patterns of speech, breathing, eye contact, and so on, and observe changes as interventions are made to increase or decrease the tension. Each intervention is consciously designed by the coach to identify the optimal level of tension. If the session feels too easy and relaxed, the coach can intervene and create more tension, to test the coachee more and challenge them to work harder.

Calibrating the coach's tension

The tension levels in the coaching room relate to both the coachee and the coach. There are two levels of tension interacting during one dialogue. Through continued personal development and self-awareness, the coach can become conscious of their own optimal level of tension. This is done again through calibration. On a very simple level, the coach can consider their emotional state at different points in the coaching session. For example:

❑ On entering the coaching session, did the coach feel comfortable, relaxed and easy, or nervous and anxious? (Self-assess on a scale of 1 to 10, 1 being completely relaxed, 10 being very anxious.)
❑ During the coaching session, did the coach notice their level of tension change? If so, what was happening at that moment?
❑ Did the coach feel uncomfortable? If so, what was happening at that moment?

137

- ❑ Did the coach feel there were times in the session that felt very relaxed? If so, what was happening at that moment?
- ❑ After the session the coach can assess their effectiveness during it (on a scale of 1 to 10, 1 being poor performance, 10 being outstanding performance) and produce a personal "performance tension model."

There is also a dynamic interaction between the coach and coachee who have different tension curves, as represented in the diagram below.

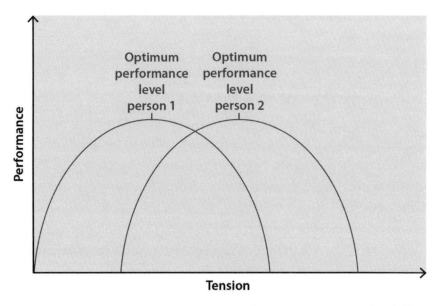

This diagram represents two people interacting with different performance curves and different optimal levels of tension. Consider the dynamics of the situation if the coach is person 1 and the coachee person 2. The coach will be working to achieve an optimal level of performance for the coachee and calibrating interventions to optimize tension. However, in our example the coachee's optimal level of tension is much greater than that of the coach. The coach may find this experience difficult as they have to move beyond their optimal level of performance. This makes for an interesting situation. How does the coach manage this level of tension for the benefit of the coachee?

The answer is in found in the coach's purpose: is the coach serving themselves or the coachee? If service of the coachee is the prime objective, then the coach must be willing to tolerate personal discomfort to optimize the coachee's performance. This is true at either end of the curve, so low tension may be uncomfortable for the coach, but optimal for the coachee. The coach will also be able to recognize and understand that stretch and exposure to tension will develop tolerance and resilience over the long term.

The dynamic management of tension

Consider how interventions by the coach can work to increase or decrease tension using both verbal and nonverbal skills.

Interventions to increase tension

- ❑ *Use of silence*—the coach asks a question or makes a statement and silence does the rest. The coachee has to ponder and think, and the coach does not intervene to give an answer or help the coachee out of a difficult situation.
- ❑ *Prolonged eye contact*—eye contact can be supportive, but prolonged eye contact can be intense, particularly when accompanying silence.
- ❑ *Probing questions*—"What else?" "What more could you do?" "What are you avoiding?" The coach does not hold back and follows their gut in probing and entering the ZOUD.
- ❑ *Challenge the coachee to take a risk*—"What is the riskiest thing you could do in this situation? Why aren't you doing it?"

- ❑ *Challenging statements*—"I think you could aim higher than that." "That sounds too easy." "There must be more." "I'm sure your boss is expecting more." "There must be something else."
- ❑ *Play devil's advocate*—start a debate and take a provocative stance.
- ❑ *Take the role of an opponent*—challenge and critique the coachee's proposed approach or action plan as if you were their most aggressive business opponent.
- ❑ *Use an approach opposite to the coachee's usual style*—if the coachee has a fast-paced active approach, the coach could force a slower pace for reflection. Alternatively, the coach could quickly move to action and not allow time for contemplation.

On a scale of 1 to 10 (10 being maximum tension), any of these interventions could increase tension from 4 to 5, but consider how these could be used to increase tension from 5 to 8. This is done by the coach not letting the coachee off the hook and being like a dog with a bone, tenacious, challenging, and provocative. This is passionate curiosity while holding the coachee accountable and honoring the contract established at the beginning of the coaching assignment. In preparation, the coach can consider the wildest and riskiest thing they could do to push the coachee; if the coach holds back then they should evaluate why they self-edited their intervention.

Interventions to decrease tension
- ❑ Increase the level of support by more active listening (summarizing, paraphrasing, and so on) and less probing.
- ❑ Acknowledge the feelings the coach is observing.
- ❑ Provide affirmation and praise.

❑ Set lower and more achievable goals so the coachee experiences the positive feelings of success.

❑ Take a break, move the coaching into a different environment, take the coaching outside the normal workplace such as walking in the open air and coaching at the same time.

❑ Move the conversation away from the topic of tension (exit the ZOUD and go back to the zone of comfortable debate).

Once the coach has calibrated the situation and suspects that tension has increased, should they immediately intervene and try to decrease the tension? Not necessarily. The skill of the coach is to spot when the coachee is becoming overloaded and their performance begins to decrease, as tension goes beyond the optimal level. Through calibration the coach can observe the signs of stress and a detrimental impact on performance.

Typical signs of stress in a coaching session are:

❑ The coachee becomes emotional and unpredictable, with a changed tone of voice.

❑ The coachee becomes aggressive and angry, displayed through a raised voice and strong language.

❑ Hesitation, disjointed sentences, loss of train of thought.

❑ Low levels of hopefulness: "I've tried that before, it won't work."

❑ The coachee becomes detached, breaks eye contact, and does not engage in the conversation.

❑ The coachee acts as if they just want to get the session over with as quickly as possible and leave the room, so agrees and nods but is really passively disagreeing.

❑ What the coachee says: "This is too much, I can't handle this right now." "I feel overwhelmed, I need to take a break."

Links to Bateson's logical levels

If tension is rising, it is a typical sign that the coachee is dealing with a big issue and that they are outside their comfort zone in an unfamiliar area that is threatening, scary, and challenging. Issues such as limiting beliefs, fear of failure, or lack of alignment with personal values can create strong emotional responses. These are subjects that relate to the essence of a person, the central core of values and beliefs that have been developed over a lifetime. These are private and vulnerable matters that when exposed can lead to an emotional and tense reaction: "a nerve has been touched," "a wound has been opened." Anthropologist Gregory Bateson described this in his work on logical levels, as represented in the diagram below.

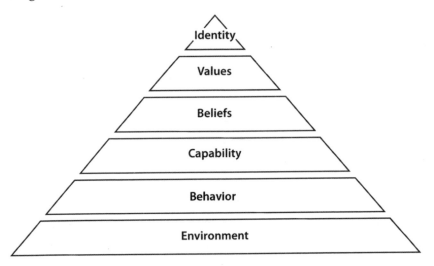

Frequently as coaches and leaders we engage with topics that are at the first three levels of environment, behavior, and capability; these are observable, clear, and relatively safe. They are outward manifestations of the deeper levels of beliefs, values, and identity. Tension is experienced when we work directly at these deeper levels, which remain more private, sensitive, and unique to each person.

The challenge for both the coach and the coachee is to use the emotional energy of tension as a catalyst and move from a thought or feeling into an action in the physical world. However, there will be resistance to change, as these values, beliefs, and feelings have been developed over many years to help the person rationalize and understand the world and, to a certain extent, to protect them. A tense and emotional response may result from the realization that a long-serving belief is actually wrong, and it takes a lot of courage to discard a belief that leads to significant resistance. A more constructive coaching approach in this situation to look at alternative beliefs and replace the old belief by asking questions such as "What do you believe to be true about...?" and by changing the perspective: "What is another interpretation of that thought?" "If you held this new belief about yourself, how would you act?" This is a process of questioning based on passionate curiosity that encourages constructive exploration, rather than a polarized "Oh yes it is... Oh no it's not..." discussion to prove or disprove a belief. Once a new belief has emerged, action will embed and reinforce the belief and the accepted new belief will replace and remove the old.

Similarly, if values are threatened, for example an action is contrary to a personal value, tension will rise. Two closely held values may be brought into conflict for an individual by an action agreed in a coaching session. For example, the value of "loyalty" may be at odds with that of "personal growth": "How can I grow as a person if that will mean breaking away from this team? How can I be so disloyal?" The coachee is in a dilemma of confusion and tension and the role of the coach is to unlock this and balance the tension. One way to do this is to look at a proposed action from the point of view of other values: "Do you want this decision to be driven by your value of loyalty, or your value of personal growth?" Consider which value is of the greatest magnitude, which value is the prime motivating force, and use that to guide the decision to act. If the number one value is maintained, tension will decrease. The coach can also ask the coachee to think of a third way: "You say that you can either have personal growth or be loyal, can you replace 'or' in that statement and use 'and'? How you can have personal growth and be loyal at the same time?" In addition, values change as we mature and life experiences influence us, so this tension may highlight an unrecognized change in beliefs. The coach is using the tension to help the coachee face the facts and speak their truth.

True transformation

In the heightened emotional state outside the comfort zone, a coachee could uncover something truly transformational. In this vulnerable space they are walking an untrodden path where they think harder, which provides the environment for a breakthrough, like the caterpillar transforming into a butterfly.

This view is supported by a number of psychological studies. For example, researchers found that workload and challenge are positively correlated to job satisfaction. Other studies have shown that psychological resilience increases through exposure to the demands of stressful experiences as people adapt and develop coping mechanisms. Another study found that intermittent stress with recovery periods leads to stress tolerance, which other psychologists have described as mental toughness, and this can be developed over time.

The orientation and skill of the coach are key to increasing or decreasing tension. If the coach believes wholeheartedly in the coachee's greatness, the tension that the coach creates will be for a positive reason. "As a coach, I believe you can achieve greatness and can do more than you currently are, and so I will push you..." In this context, the tension created by coaching is constructive. This is completely different to an overbearing or bullying line manager who increases tension for their own reasons relating to status, power, or control, which is aimed at belittling an individual.

Imagine a coaching session in which the coachee role plays being the chief executive who has to make a decision about a new way of structuring the organization. The coach puts the coachee in the chief executive's position and says, "OK, if it was your business, what would you do?" The coachee replies, "I don't know what I'd do." The coach responds, "You've got to make a decision, you're the boss." Following this intervention, the coach falls silent and allows the tension in the session to rise as the coachee grapples with the ultimatum they have been given. Eventually, the coachee declares, "I've got it! It isn't about the structure at all. No structure would resolve this problem—we just need to work better as a team and that's where I want to focus my energy." If coaches hold the view that tension is negative and destructive and should be avoided at all costs, they might be selling their coachees short.

To clarify, we are not advocating throwing someone in at the deep end; this approach is not "sink or swim." However, we are also not advocating holding the person safe and protecting them in a comfort zone that limits their potential. We are saying that well-managed tension is constructive and leads to transformation. Coaches should not protect or seek to rescue their coachees, but they should allow them to grow and develop mental toughness—to be all that they can be.

EXERCISES

1   Create a tension graph using the template below. Reflect on coaching sessions or any other meetings when you felt the tension build.

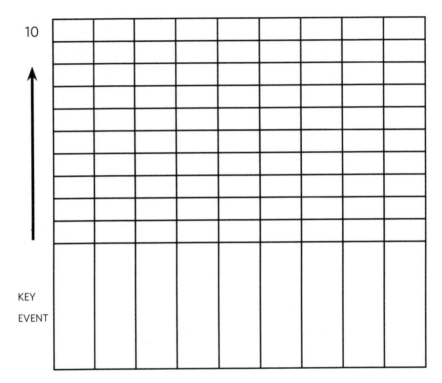

☐   Plot on the graph the level of tension from 1 to 10 (10 being maximum level of tension).

☐   In the Key Event section note what was happening at the time.

☐   What did you do with the tension and how did you react?

☐   What are the themes and common features in your examples?

☐   What does this tell you?

Discuss with a trusted colleague or friend your thoughts and reflections on how you respond to tension and the impact this has on your coaching.

2   In coaching pairs, discuss a controversial topic and take opposing views. For example, Person A starts the discussion with the statement "Barack Obama is a great President because..." Person B responds with "I disagree, because..." Allow the disagreement to take place and deliberately be proactive, argumentative, and confrontational (this is an exercise, play with the tension) and continue for a few minutes, then pause and review what happened. How do you and the other person feel? Did you try to reduce the tension; if so when, why and how? What impact has this had on your relationship?

FACTS example dialogue

A managing director, Samra, has received negative feedback from her colleagues regarding the performance of her sales and marketing director, Brian. While Brian is delivering stunning results, he is considered to be a poor communicator. In particular, he is perceived to show disrespect for his seniors, avoiding opportunities to share information and appearing rude when in meetings and conference calls.

Samra believes that Brian is being naïve about the politics of the organization, risking his future progression despite his obvious potential. Brian's view is that the organization is ridden with politics and has no respect for the culture of senior management. His self-confidence is such that he is prepared to leave the organization and get a new role rather than "play the game."

With Brian's full support, Samra has engaged a coach. In the initial three-way contracting discussion, Samra states that she expects Brian to shift the perceptions of key senior managers in a month via a blitz of communication activity. She has even drafted the contents of this communication prior to the meeting and presents these to Brian as a fait accompli. Brian does not react and appears very accepting of Samra's expectations.

However, at the first one-to-one coaching session while discussing the goals and measures of success for the coaching program, it becomes clear that Brian has not bought into the goals Samra has presented. Where does the coach go from here when following the FACTS approach?

The FACTS response

[At this point the coach takes a step back to calibrate the tension that exists for Brian in this situation. While in theory this is a situation in which many executives would feel great pressure due to the negative feedback and the high expectations, the coach realizes that Brian is not feeling this pressure and has a laid-back attitude. In response to this the coach decides to ramp up the tension.]

> COACH: It is clear to me that you are not committed to the goals that Samra has set for this coaching and yet you did not openly challenge these goals in our three-way meeting. As your coach, I am unable to commit to this assignment because I do not believe we have the conditions to deliver a win/win solution for you and your employer.
>
> COACHEE: [leaning forward and appearing more engaged] But your role is to support me in this process, to help me improve my communication skills.
>
> COACH: I am here to challenge you to achieve the goals we identified and only if I believe that we have alignment between your goals and those of the sponsor of this coaching, namely Samra. Currently, I do not think you are being honest with Samra about your reaction to

her expectations. I'm not interested in being part of a covert operation to pay lip service to Samra's expectations and creating an alternative agenda.

[The tension has jumped to another level but is not yet red lining. The coach realizes that the coachee can handle this level of tension and that it is provoking him to think and to engage.]

COACHEE: Well, how do you suggest we handle this, then?

[The agitation in the coachee's voice gives the coach a clue that they are at risk of losing the rapport to an extent that may be damaging to the relationship. However, through the calibration the coach believes that the coachee is robust and able to take this high level of tension, so holds it at the current level.]

COACH: I'm not sure. What do you think would be a win/win outcome for both you and Samra in this situation?

[Right now, the atmosphere in the coaching session is heavy with tension and frustration. Part of the coach wants to make things easier by offering a suggestion or backing off from the original position, or by changing the subject and asking where the toilets are! However, after what seems like an eternity, the coachee turns and looks the coach in the eye.

COACHEE: I need to go back to Samra and let her know that her expectations for this coaching work are unrealistic. I want to renegotiate the goals and measures of success with her and get to a place where we have a shared agenda.

[The coach sits back and lets out all the tension in the system with an audible sigh of relief.]

> COACH: Good, it feels to me as though you are facing the facts and speaking your truth. On that basis we can work together. Now let's plan for your conversation with Samra.

[The coaching session continues, but now on a very different path.]

CHAPTER 8
FACTS—Systems thinking

How do we know all this? Because we know that each part is in the whole and the whole is in each part. (Tao Te Ching, Verse 54)

Last but not least we reach the "S" of FACTS, which represents systems thinking, a skill very different to any of those we have discussed in the model so far and yet inextricably linked to all of them. We use the phrase systems thinking to describe the belief that everything in the world is connected and that it is the relationship between things rather than the things themselves that is the primary determinant of desirable or undesirable outcomes. While systems thinking is a discipline that has existed for many years and was brought into the mainstream of business thinking via books like *The Fifth Discipline* by Peter Senge, it seems that it is still regarded as an academic concept and not a principle by which people should live or coaches should conduct their work.

In this chapter we use the language and paradigm of systems thinking to create a deeper awareness of how a coach can make a positive difference to individuals, but also leverage this impact to influence the wider organization to the benefit of all stakeholders. We take a short tour of the concepts of the systems thinking world, mapping these to the skills of the FACTS coach, and exploring how a systems-centered approach to coaching can increase its impact and its reach. We introduce the idea of "dancing with the system"—listening at a deeply intuitive level and responding on behalf of the system's will, insight, and purpose. Finally, we assess how a focus on systems thinking links back to the other skills in the FACTS approach and binds them

151

into a consistent perspective. In doing so we refer frequently to a seminal text that has informed our work in this area: Donella Meadows' *Systems Thinking*. For those who wish to pursue this topic further, we particularly recommend Chapters 1, 2, 6, and 7 of Donella's book.

As a starting definition, we can regard any system as "an interconnected set of elements that is coherently organized in way that achieves something." The human body is a system. Its elements are the various organs, muscles, bones, and so on. These are interconnected via the flow of blood, the nervous system, and physical tissue. The purpose of the human body is to keep the organism healthy, safe, and conscious. Similarly, a business organization is a system. Its elements are the people who work in it, its customers, its shareholders, and so on. It is interconnected via various flows of information, materials, and money. Its purpose is to deliver goods and/or services that are valuable to society in a way that generates financial returns for its various stakeholders. All systems share some common characteristics and some rules of behavior that we investigate via a series of concepts.

Systems thinking concept I: Suboptimization

One of the first implications of systems thinking is the awareness that systems are often embedded in other systems, which are themselves further embedded in yet other systems. Hence the definition of the boundary of a system depends on the perspective we are adopting at any point in time. This nesting of systems is shown in the diagram opposite. The system that is "I" is nested within the system that is the team, which is nested in the function, the organization, the private/public sector, the country, and so on.

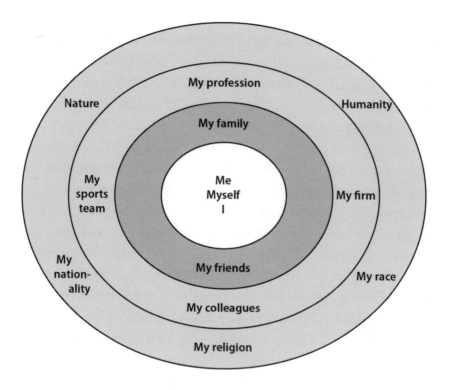

When a coach is working with one individual it can be tempting to think of that individual as an island and to consider that their actions are independent of what is happening in the rest of the organization. This is a person-centered approach, not a systems thinking approach. In systems thinking the risk that the goals at a subsystem level dominate at the expense of the total system's goals is known as suboptimization.

A good example of suboptimization occurred in the banking sector in the early 2000s when bank traders were allowed to pursue the goal of maximizing their personal bonuses irrespective of the wider consequences of their actions. There were many high-profile cases of traders who took this approach to the limit and jeopardized the viability of the entire organization. As this behavior spread, it was ultimately the collation of all these examples of suboptimization that led to a breakdown in the global banking system itself.

Suboptimization occurs in coaching when the individual's goals are achieved, but at the expense of broader goals related to the individual's team, department, or wider organization. To reduce this risk in the FACTS coaching approach, we place a much greater emphasis on mapping the nest of systems in which the individual is operating and contracting with each stakeholder that emerges from this perspective.

We came across an example of suboptimization in a coaching context when working with the managing director of a division of a global IT organization. The MD's team felt very comfortable with their immediate leader and believed they were delivering excellent results. There was a high level of trust between the MD and the immediate team, and from the perspective of the business unit level it appeared that all was well. However, when working with the team as coaches it appeared increasingly evident that the business unit subsystem was being optimized at the expense of the wider organizational goals. More senior stakeholders were being prevented from having input to the coaching program and their negative views on the business unit's performance were being dismissed as irrelevant and motivated by personal attack rather than an objective assessment of the situation.

As coaches in this situation it is easy to collude with the subsystem perspective, because it is more immediately comfortable to align with these stakeholders against the common enemy of the big, bad management above. To be able to step back, see the bigger picture, and then feed back this perspective as an independent third eye is to take a systems thinking perspective and to act on behalf of the wider good. In this example, as trust was built we increasingly challenged the prevailing view of the MD and her team and shared facts and information that supported a different perspective. As this happened, the tension in the situation increased and individual coaching sessions became more challenging. The situation came to a head when the MD agreed to engage their own boss in a more honest and challenging conversation about the realities of the situation. Ultimately, this conversation resulted in a surprising win/win outcome for all stakeholders. A new MD was appointed, but this happened through a proactive plan that was agreed with the existing MD and allowed her to leave the organization with her dignity and financial security intact. The team's performance improved since they were no longer operating in denial of the wider system reality. Ironically, the new MD was not a fan of coaching and our assignment ended shortly after his appointment.

Systems thinking concept II: Emergence

Emergence is the idea that complex systems have the capacity to exhibit new behaviors and that such behaviors can be triggered by small changes in the detail of the situation. This is popularly known as the "butterfly effect," after experiments by Edward Lorenz in 1961. Lorenz researched weather patterns and discovered that a change of only one part in a thousand to the set of numbers he typed into his weather simulation programs could produce dramatically different weather system patterns that grew further and further apart. He concluded that in theory, a butterfly flapping its wings in South America could trigger a tornado in Japan via emergent developments in the complex system that is the global weather.

Likewise, whenever we coach in a corporate context, we become an active part of that wider organizational system. It is one thing for us to be confidential, independent, and detached, but this does not mean we can ignore the wider impacts of our work. How do you know that the flapping of your coaching wings might not shift the energy in the system in such a way that significant impacts emerge from your interventions? To believe this is possible is both an exciting prospect and a serious responsibility.

Systems thinking concept III: Fractals

The term "fractal" is used to describe how the examination of a small-scale component of a system can reveal information relating to the system as a whole. This term was originated by mathematical physicist Benoît Mandelbrot, who used it to describe naturally occurring irregular shapes where the degree of irregularity or fragmentation is identical at all scales. A popular example is the coastline of a country, which has lookalike features and characteristics whether viewed close up or at a distance and whose features, while highly irregular, can still be described using complicated mathematical formulae and definitions. Others intuited the concept of fractals long before they were scientifically defined—when English poet William Blake wrote "to see the whole world in a grain of sand" in the poem "Auguries of Innocence" he was poetically referring to the idea of fractals.

In *Adventures in Complexity*, Lesley Kuhn concludes that in an organizational context, fractals are helpful in understanding processes and potentialities. If organizations are fractal in nature, then we can choose our focus of investigation knowing that one area of focus will contain information about all other levels. Similarly, we need to recognize that the feelings, behavior, and attitudes of individuals will be replicated throughout the organization in teams, departments, divisions, and so on; what is commonly termed organizational culture.

Hence, in coaching an individual at a personal level, much will also be revealed about the nature of the organizational system since they represent a fractal of that organization. A vivid example of this occurred when we were coaching at two different management levels of a Scandinavian telecommunications company. At the more senior level, a director had been talking about the risk that the organization would "hit the wall" due to the extent of its ambition and the pace at which this was being pursued. At the lower level, his direct report had hit the wall physically in recent months due to excessive stress and was being coached back into full performance. When the link between the two areas of focus was raised in the awareness of both stakeholders by the coach, it led to some dramatic and positive outcomes. One of the coachees even commented that they felt this was a pattern within the Scandinavian culture as a whole, thus alluding to the relevance of the fractal at a system level above and beyond the organization itself.

Systems thinking concept IV: Leverage points

The phrase leverage points is used in systems thinking to describe those points in the system where tension is being held and the subtle release of this tension will lead to dramatic results. An example can be seen in the practice of martial arts. How is it that a wiry, 7 stone t'ai chi master can throw a 6 foot 3 hulk across the room with seemingly no great effort at all? The t'ai chi master has spent a lifetime studying human leverage points. They instinctively sense when the opponent is fractionally off balance and use this opportunity to intervene decisively, employing the weight of the other person to create a dramatic momentum. This is the meaning of the t'ai chi phrase "a force of four ounces deflects a thousand pounds."

In coaching, leverage points in the system may be specific individuals who have become talismanic within the organization. They could also be specific moments of time when the system is poised on a decision point that will have far-reaching and irreversible repercussions. They could also exist in relation to limiting beliefs and assumptions that the system has bred over time but are now holding back the next stage of its development. If a coach is sensitive to such leverage points and bold enough to intervene decisively when the moment arises, a disproportionate impact can be created akin to the impact of a martial arts expert on a larger, stronger opponent.

The role of intuition

Having briefly toured the systems thinking world, you may have quickly reached the conclusion that organizational systems of this type are far too complex to be understood and analyzed by the rational mind. Self-organizing, nonlinear, messy, and dynamic organizational systems defy our tendency to want to control and structure and predict behavior. The only human faculty with the speed and accuracy to discern and navigate within such complexity is intuition. In the context of coaching, it is intuition that allows a coach to make pinpoint interventions that not only shift the individual, but also have the potential to move the whole system.

If intuition is the key to unlocking a systems-centered approach, then how can a coach hone their intuition? How can a coach dance with the system to create a dynamic relationship with the wider whole, engaging it consciously and proactively through the course of working with only a handful of individual leaders?

Using a simple metaphor, as experienced ballroom dancers glide across the dance floor a graceful exchange is occurring. One leads, the other follows. One rises, one falls. One steps forward, the other steps back. There is great trust and respect and a harmony of movement that surpasses what either could achieve by themselves. What does it take to be a great dancer? What does it take to dance with the system as a coach?

To answer these questions we will introduce three critical skills:

❑ Sensitive listening
❑ Systems-centered questions
❑ Giving the system a voice

Sensitive listening

In *Co-Active Coaching*, Whitworth, Kimsey-House, and Sandahl introduced the concept of Level III listening, otherwise known as global listening. They suggest that Level I listening is internal listening, primarily focused on one's own thoughts, feelings, and opinions. Level II listening they termed focused listening, characterized by a sharp focus on the other person: the words they use, their expressions, their feelings. They suggested that most coaches exhibit Level II listening and challenged them to stretch to a Level III mode. While they did not link Level III listening directly to a systems thinking approach, it is interesting to note the language they used in describing it:

> *At Level III, you listen as though you and the client were at the center of the Universe receiving information from everywhere at once. It is as though you were surrounded by a force field that contains you, the client and the space of knowing. If Level II is hardwired then Level III is like a radio field.*

In the FACTS approach, sensitive listening is Level III listening. It is listening to the system of which the coach and coachee are part. It is a profound sensitivity to the unspoken and subtle levels of information that flow unconsciously in any situation. This is not information that today can be scientifically verified, but Whitworth and colleagues liken it to radio waves. Radio waves are invisible, yet music emerges from a radio if it has a suitable antenna and is tuned to the right frequency. Marconi proved the existence of radio waves, but they still existed before they were scientifically proven; sometimes we have to trust the evidence of our experience before it's been scientifically proven.

Examples of sensitive listening in coaching include:

❑ "I don't know about you, but I just got a sense that your dilemma is not only about you but is representative of broader challenges in this organization."
❑ "When you used the word 'panic' I felt a deep impact from that word and I'm wondering what that's all about. What did you feel?"
❑ "I just had a picture come into my mind of a tree that's been uprooted by a storm. Does that picture mean anything to you in this situation?"
❑ "I'm seeing a pattern here whereby the organization is trying to shift its culture over a period of years but failing at the same point each time. You are the latest leader whom it believes might be able to facilitate this change. What personal step for you might lead to this wider transformation in the organization?"

Sensitive listening requires extreme concentration and quietness of mind. It is as if the coach momentarily loses their sense of self-identity and is consumed by the wider system identity. At this point, the coach receives privileged access to information that is lying below the level of consciousness of the individuals involved. In Jungian terms, at this point we are going beyond the personal consciousness and tapping into what he referred to as the collective unconscious. Jung believed that the collective unconscious was part of the unconscious mind, expressed in humanity and all life forms. He distinguished the collective unconscious from the personal unconscious, in that the personal unconscious is a personal reservoir of experience unique to each individual, while the collective unconscious collects and organizes those personal experiences in a similar way with each member of a particular species. As he put it:

> *My thesis then, is as follows: in addition to our immediate consciousness, which is of a thoroughly personal nature and which we believe to be the only empirical psyche, there exists a second psychic system of a collective, universal, and impersonal nature which is identical in all individuals. This collective unconscious does not develop individually but is inherited. It consists of pre-existent forms, the archetypes, which can only become conscious secondarily and which give definite form to certain psychic contents.*

Systems-centered questions

Alongside switching on our Level III global listening antennae, we also recommend the use of powerful, systems-centered questions that raise the coachee's self-awareness of the wider implications of their thinking and behavior. Such questions are designed to broaden the coachee's sphere of responsibility. While these are definitely leading questions, they do not assume that the coach knows the right answer, although they do challenge the coachee to expand their thinking.

The diagram on page 153 gives us a map of possible perspectives from which to ask powerful, systems-centered questions. Such questions prompt the coachee to shift their level of thinking and look at the issue from a broader perspective. For example, you might be working with a coachee on the topic of their work/life balance. Questions that ask the coachee to consider the perspective of their family as well as their boss on such a topic are already bringing into play different stakeholders in the system.

Or you might be working with a coachee on a sensitive decision that involves a tradeoff between profit and people. A simple question such as "If your decision were to be featured tomorrow on the front page of the *Daily Telegraph*, how would you feel?" confronts the coachee to bring in the perspective of the general public, their friends, and their family, and so could shift their focus to many different levels of the system.

In the FACTS approach, we encourage coaches to create powerful questions that invite the coachee to explore the systems impact of their thinking from the following stakeholder perspectives:

- ❑ Customers
- ❑ Staff
- ❑ Shareholders
- ❑ Society
- ❑ Family
- ❑ Friends

Example coaching questions for each of these stakeholder perspectives include:

❑ "How do you think your customers would react to this?"
❑ "In this situation, what could you do that would make your staff feel very proud to work for you and this company?"
❑ "If you owned this business, how would that change your thinking?"
❑ "If you were being profiled in the media as a great business leader, how would you like to be portrayed?"
❑ "Who in your family might be able to bring a valuable perspective to this challenge?"
❑ "Who is your best friend? What would their advice be to you right now?"

This is not an exhaustive list and each coach will find their own versions of these questions in the moment with their coachee. The purpose of the FACTS approach is to raise the coaching profession's own awareness of its role in the wider system and invite coaches to take responsibility for this without compromising their nonjudgmental stance. You could view it as the coaching profession's contribution to the sustainability agenda!

Armed with the skills of sensitive listening and powerful systems-centered questions, the coach starts to get the beat of the organizational system. They begin to build a relationship with the system as well as the individual. A picture starts to form that is always incomplete, always changing, yet nevertheless becoming a resource to support ongoing work. The coach starts to see a fractal of the wider system in the individual and they begin to map this fractal onto other levels of the system of which they are part. The coach then senses the limits in the system, its purpose, the edges where it is striving to develop, the flows of energy and where this might be blocked, the leverage points and where these are located. This is all an imprecise, intuitive presence, yet one in which the coach engages proactively and consciously.

After working with one of our client organizations for over five years, it became clear to us when listening in this way that the organizational system was striving to evolve from a national, individualistic culture to a global, corporate entity. To achieve this, individuals had been promoted into key leadership roles (leverage points) from different country backgrounds and different experience bases to the norm. Working with these individuals as coaches, it was clear that they were feeling the tension of embodying personally the system's wider purpose (fractals). The reactions they received from other stakeholders were emotional and dramatic (the butterfly effect). They were tempted to take these reactions personally until, working with a coach, they gained a systems perspective, becoming aware of the nest of systems of which they were a part and seeing the bigger picture of their symbolic part in the system's emergent possibilities.

Giving the system a voice

For those with a rational mind, this next section will prove challenging, since none of what we share here has been proven by science. It is an experiential text, an intuitive explanation of intuitive moments. For those with a spiritual faith, the section may chime with religious concepts and beliefs, since all of what we say can be likened to a relationship of trust and love with a higher power. Therefore, read it according to your own frame of reference. Make of it what you will. Do not try to understand or critically appraise it, but rather assess how it makes you feel and play with it as an imaginative possibility that may create a new perspective on your current view of reality.

Imagine for a moment that the system of which you are part is a living entity with a will and a purpose and resources and power. In the evolving dance with the wider system, it is as if the system itself slowly builds trust in you. It tests you by revealing information that could be used in your self-interest: progressively more sensitive disclosure of the full reality of the rational, emotional, and spiritual road map of the host organization. There are often moments when what is seen as not uplifting or desirable breaks to the surface of consciousness and waits to see if it will be judged, abandoned, or attacked. The system is like an individual in that it has its shadow, its imperfect history, its hopes, and its failed dreams.

As trust develops, the system grants you its power and invites you to speak on its behalf. It can be profoundly unnerving to be sat in the midst of a coaching conversation and it is as if someone else takes over the controls momentarily and, with absolute authority and knowing, says, "Do this now!" Your rational mind, usurped from its customary position of power and control, rebels against this rude interruption and replies, "You're joking! There's no way I'm saying that or doing that. It doesn't make any sense at all." Of course it doesn't make sense, it's the voice of your intuition. It's the mysterious link that your right brain is able to make with the wider system it instinctively serves.

In FACTS coaching, when these moments happen you swallow hard and you speak. However absurd the idea, feeling, or thought it is not held back: it is trusted and it is shared. In this moment, the coach steps into the unknown, lets go, and allows what wants to happen... just to happen. Whatever wants to come through you from the wider system is given free passage and the coach in this moment is merely acting as the hollow container that enables the unspoken to be spoken.

It may help at this point to discuss an example. We experienced a coaching session where the topic was a possible job change. The coachee could not understand why more was not happening to enable such a change to take place. He was frustrated and beginning to raise the stakes with his existing manager about his desire for a change in a certain timescale and the possibility of him leaving if something did not happen. Out of the blue, in the midst of a great deal of angst, the coach had an urge and an intuition to throw in the phrase "Not now!" These two simple words hit the coachee like a steam train and carried an inspired authority that was very evident to both the coach and the client. This was a very directive statement that in the wrong context and with the wrong tone could have provoked a negative reaction in the coachee. But in the context of intuitive words inspired by an awareness of the wider system and offered without judgment or attachment, this intervention left the coachee dumbfounded and with tears in his eyes. After a long period of silence in which both were aware of great emotions rising up and then falling away, the coachee, who later declared himself a devout Christian, said, "I think I just experienced a God moment."

Whatever language we choose to describe these experiences, there's no escaping their power and impact if you're in their presence. Everyone knows that something important has just happened, yet no one can say exactly what. It's precisely because of this power that there is, for many, a temptation to hold back, edit, and censor such outbursts. After all, who are we to speak with such seeming authority? It feels almost blasphemous and it would be if the intention behind it were not a pure desire to be in service to the system and its highest purpose in that moment. Put it this way: the system knows what you can handle, it knows for what purpose it can use you and what your limits are. Trust it.

The great irony of the two skills of sensitive listening and giving the system a voice is that those who are naturally gifted at the first often find the second profoundly difficult and vice versa. However, if those who can hear the system do not speak and if those who cannot hear the system do speak, then what inevitably follows is an authority vacuum in which all parties are culpable and the system inevitably stalls in its evolution.

Donella Meadows suggests in her book that, based on her years of study of complex systems, she would add an eleventh commandment to the ten that already exist: "Thou shalt not distort, delay, or withhold information." It may have been a lighthearted metaphor, yet it hints at the profound necessity of not holding back on the insights and intuition the system may grant you and ask you to share in your work. Be brave!

Links to other FACTS principles and skills

While it is the last letter of our FACTS acronym, the "S" of systems thinking permeates and binds all other aspects of this coaching approach. As you have read this chapter you may have already instinctively started to link this topic to the other components. Here is a brief summary of how the links occur using quotes from Donella Meadows' book where appropriate.

Feedback

Missing information flows are one of the most common causes of system malfunction... it is important that missing feedback be restored to the right place and in compelling form.

The coach is in a privileged position to play this role in an organizational system by giving feedback to individuals, as described in Chapter 4. In so doing, the individual benefits but the wider system benefits as well, as vital information is freely shared with specific detail but without judgment. Coaches in this mode act as guardians of the system's best interests, they observe fractal realities through sensitive listening, and then they are bold to share these observations with key stakeholders.

Accountability

There is a systematic tendency on the part of human beings to avoid accountability for their own decisions... a great deal of responsibility was lost when rulers who declared war were no longer expected to lead their troops into battle.

Subsystems and the individuals within them create their own behavior, but often detach themselves from facing the full consequences of their actions. In particular, it suits leaders to stay in denial regarding the wider collateral damage of their behavior to other stakeholders in the larger nest of systems.

For example, we are only now holding the world of business accountable for its impact on the environment and creating measures for this, such as carbon footprints. In the future we expect this trend toward transparency and measurement to increase to cover a broader range of currently hidden system impacts. As highlighted by a recent *Harvard Business Review* article, "Leadership in the Age of Transparency," "the key to becoming a contemporary corporate leader is to take on responsibility for externalities—what economists call the impacts you have on the world (like pollution) for which you are not yet called to account." We see it as an important part of the role of a FACTS coach to restore responsibility to its source through the holding of accountability at the three levels discussed in Chapter 5.

Courageous goals

Two of the prime leverage points in a system are its goals and its purpose. The thermostat of a central heating system sets the goal of the system. Intervention at this level, for example to change the desired temperature, has knock-on effects on the entire system: boilers are fired, pumps start working, water starts flowing, and heat is generated in specific places at specific times. Leaders in organizations set goals and targets. Top leaders also define the purpose and mission. Working as a coach with such leaders to raise awareness around the system's highest purpose and challenging them to reach courageously for this is a fundamental systems-centered intervention. Like the temperature of a heating thermostat, the goals of an organization have a knock-on effect on the entire system: staff are recruited, processes are put in place, goods and services are provided, and profits are generated in specific places and at specific times.

Tension

Tension, as discussed in Chapter 7, relates to the system thinking concept of limits. Every system has its limits and its optimal range of effective operation. For the system that is the human body, the optimal temperature is 98.4°F. At this temperature the efficiency of the system is optimized. In a fever, the temperature will rise or drop unpredictably, leading to fatigue and uncomfortable side effects. As the limits of the coaching relationship are explored the tension will wax and wane. The skill of the coach is to test these limits dynamically using the coachee's responses as their guide rather than their own level of comfort or discomfort.

Build the contract, honor the contract

Referring back to Chapter 3 and the introduction of the two new gems of FACTS coaching principles, we can also see a link to the world of systems thinking. Contracts capture rules and the consequences of breaking them. In systems thinking, rules define the scope, boundaries, and degrees of freedom of the system and its elements. Rules are powerful: they are high leverage points in systems. Change the rules and you change the game. For example, in the reaction to the financial crisis, political governments around the world were forced to reflect on the rules of the game for the financial services sector. A lax regulatory environment had allowed the rules to be defined to the benefit of one group of stakeholders (bank traders) and at the expense of others (shareholders, taxpayers). Through the legal framework the rules of the financial sector can be changed, whether that be through taxation, structural break-ups, greater policing, and so on.

Similarly, in FACTS coaching the rules of the coaching game must be clearly negotiated up front and honored throughout the engagement. If not, the coach loses their integrity as an agent of system-wide change. This is a view of coaching that challenges the profession to establish its own self-regulation or risk external intervention.

Speak your truth, face the FACTS

The first step in respecting language is to keep it as concrete, meaningful and truthful as possible... If something is ugly say so. If it is tacky, inappropriate, out of proportion, unsustainable, ecologically impoverishing or humanly demeaning don't let it pass.

Systems are liberated by the truth. Coaches who care will hold this as an absolute standard in their work.

Our tour of the systems-centered world and its link to FACTS has revealed the potential power and impact of this approach. There is a risk that this power tempts the coach to step over the line between coaching and mentoring/consulting. There is also a risk that a FACTS coach slips into judgment around "what the system wants"; that is, they start believing that they know the big answers to the big questions and think that their role is to impose this worldview on the coachee regardless of the coachee's own values and perspectives. An element of persuasion and manipulation could creep into the situation if the coach does not stay in a place of humility.

At a leading coaching conference, we participated in a keynote panel discussion on the topics raised in this chapter. The debate provoked a well-known coaching figure to declare: "Who do we think we are? It isn't our job to save the banks or to save society." This is true: it isn't the job of a FACTS coach to save anyone or anything. The temptation to step into this role must be guarded against as the coach becomes more confident in their presence and skills.

An example would be a coach who is passionate about the environment and who allows this passion to show up in their coaching in a way that uses a subtle guilt trip to manipulate a coachee's outlook and actions. The more involved in a situation we become, the greater the risk that what started as honest intuition and sensitive listening becomes distorted into judgment and prejudice. The FACTS coach recognizes this risk and recontracts on a regular basis to ensure that they are holding themselves accountable to the integrity of their approach.

This said, we do feel that it is the role of a challenging, FACTS coach to ask difficult systems thinking questions, to represent the view of hidden stakeholders, to hold accountability in its widest interpretation, and to use all these tools to raise the collective awareness of all stakeholders. To the extent that coaches and leaders do this, then to the same extent we can expect the world of business to achieve its most courageous goals and unlock its utmost potential as a positive agent of change in the world.

EXERCISES

1   With a fellow coach, discuss the implications of a systems think-
    ing approach for the skills needed to be an effective executive
    coach. What does this say about the development of your coach-
    ing skills?

2   Again with a trusted fellow coach or colleague, practice not holding
    back. Begin a co-coaching session and give each other permission
    to speak very freely. Forget the old rule that the coachee should
    speak more than the coach, just let it happen. This is practice so
    that you begin to feel comfortable saying whatever comes to mind
    regardless.
    ❑   As the coachee talks the coach is free to say anything, the
        coach speaks every thought that comes to mind, there is no
        self-censorship or editing.
    ❑   The coach should practice listening to words, tone of voice,
        being aware of posture and pauses, and engaging intuition
        and gut feeling.
    ❑   What do the words that are being spoken by the coachee and
        the way they are being spoken suggest about the bigger sys-
        tem of which they are part?

3   Begin a co-coaching session with a trusted colleague. During the
    session, encourage the coachee to thing about all the stakeholders
    who are involved in this situation. Encourage the coachee to think
    about immediate stakeholders and less obvious stakeholders who
    may be affected at a later date. Ask how each stakeholder would
    look at this situation and about their perspective. Finally, consider
    action for the coachee to take based on this. Use a flipchart to
    record these thoughts, as in the example opposite.

Stakeholder	When they may be affected	How will this stakeholder look at this situation? What is their perspective on this matter?
1		
2		
3		
Etc.		
Action based on this...		

4   Great chess players plan their moves in advance. Bring to mind a clear action that you want to take, which can be anything where there is a clear intention to act. Consider the first step you will take: what will be the likely outcome for you and other stakeholders? Based on this, what is your next step? Again, consider possible outcomes for you and other stakeholders. Continue, challenge yourself to go further, then evaluate: does the outcome achieve the outcome that you and other stakeholders desire? You have dropped a pebble into the pond, where do the ripples go?

	Action Step 1	Outcome Step 1	Action Step 2	Outcome Step 2	Etc.
Me					
Stakeholder 1					
Stakeholder 2					

5   Begin a co-coaching session with five chairs in a circle, one each for you and a colleague who will be your coachee, and three empty chairs.

   ❏   Ask the coachee to consider the world from the perspective of a stakeholder and to sit in one of the empty chairs. What would the stakeholder say to the coachee? The coachee speaks the words as if they were the stakeholder.

   ❏   Ask the coachee to move to another empty chair. What would someone completely detached from this situation say? Speak the words again as the neutral observer.

   ❏   Ask the coachee to move to the final empty chair, which is placed in the future. Consider the long-term impacts of the situation. The coachee should speak the words as if they have been projected forward in time, six months, twelve months, five years—whichever is suitable.

   ❏   The coachee returns to their original chair. What has this told them?

FACTS example dialogue

You have been approached by a major UK organization to coach a newly appointed senior leader, Katherine. In the criteria for selecting you as her coach, Katherine stresses that she is particularly interested in your spiritual outlook and wants you to bring this to the coaching engagement alongside your business experience. The focus of the coaching program is building confidence in the first 100 days of the new role.

In the first session, it soon becomes clear that Katherine is surprised to have been promoted and has found herself in a very challenging political environment. She is even questioning whether the organization made the right decision in promoting her, since she feels like a fish out of water in the new role. Confidence is ebbing away as she haunts herself with the thought that she and the organization have made a big mistake. Where do you go from here if you are following the FACTS approach?

[When Katherine states that she feels like "a fish out of water," this is communicating to you that she does not feel at home in the current system. Therefore, using the FACTS approach, it triggers your systems thinking awareness and encourages you to explore the context further.]

> COACH: What do you think is your purpose in this political system?
> COACHEE: To change it.
> COACH: And when you were chosen for the role, what do you think your new boss was expecting of you?

[Coach seeks the line manager's perspective via a systems thinking question.]

> COACHEE: To change the current way of doing things.
> COACH: So it seems that you and your boss agree that your role is to change this system and therefore I am not surprised that you feel like a fish out of water right now. What is your highest vision for the reason you are a change agent in this system?

[This question invites the coachee to expand their thinking several levels further out from their immediate system level.]

> COACHEE: I believe that people want a different style of leadership in the world right now. I think they are

sick of the old ways and are demanding that organizations like ours reinvent themselves to present a more human, caring, authentic face to the world.

[At this stage, the coachee is tapping into a deep, personal purpose and drawing strength and confidence from the vision she holds around leadership. She is sensing that she is not alone and that many others share this vision, even though they might not be in her immediate political system.]

> COACH: And do you feel like a fish out of water now?
> COACHEE: No, not from that perspective. From that perspective I feel part of an inspiring movement of people and I can understand why this is exactly the right role for me to be doing right now.
> COACH: And what do you want your grandchildren to say about you when they speak of your time as a leader in business?
> COACHEE: I want them to feel proud of me, to know that I was brave, and that I had a vision, and that I pursued it despite the obstacles and barriers along the way. I want them to think that I was part of the solution and not part of the problem.

[The sense of a shift in the coachee's confidence is palpable at this point in the coaching session. Reconnecting with her wider purpose and vision has empowered her. As coach, you can now work with this empowerment to generate action and commitment.]

> COACH: Who else can support you in this role now that you have seen a higher purpose?

COACHEE: Well, I would never have thought of this before, but I can see that spending time with Peter, my old boss who now heads up the accounts function, would be very helpful. Peter shares my vision and is a change agent in his own way. I will arrange to have lunch with him and use this as an opportunity to compare notes on how we view the organization right now.

COACH: And how about your boss, what feels like the next step in that relationship?

COACHEE: I am 90 percent sure that my boss recruited me to be a change agent, but it would help me to have the conversation directly with him to eliminate that final 10 percent of doubt in my mind. I've been avoiding this conversation for fear that I might have got the wrong end of the stick, but I can now see that this is just leaving me in "no man's land."

COACH: Great! Your vision is inspiring and it sounds like you're in exactly the right place at exactly the right time.

CHAPTER 9
Applying the FACTS

The best leader is indistinguishable from the will of those who selected him or her. (Tao Te Ching, Verse 17)

In the previous chapters we have discussed the FACTS model in detail to explain the concept and approach of challenging coaching. In this chapter we focus more on the practical application of FACTS on a day-to-day basis from the perspective of a leader. As well as being writers and coaches we are also business people, so everything we do must make a difference. Everything we do has to have a purpose to improve the performance of individuals, teams, and organizations. This book has been written not as an intellectual discussion, but as a practical guide. As one colleague frequently said, "This is where the rubber hits the road."

In addition to coaching, the FACTS approach has real application in other areas of business leadership. The art of leadership is challenging. There are many demands and time constraints on leaders that mean they don't always have 1–2 hours to dedicate to coaching; instead, the leader must catch 10–20-minute conversations with multiple direct reports to maximize the effectiveness of the individual, team, and organization. There are no right or wrong answers in leadership, no formulae to follow. In business there are a vast number of variables, too many to contemplate and certainly too many to control or influence. So the quality of leadership depends heavily on the judgment of the individual leader in a particular situation, with a particular person, at a particular time. Given this, a leader needs a strong basis for making decisions and the FACTS principles provide this framework. In this chapter we look at the common leadership challenges of delegation, performance management, personal objective setting, managing upward, client interactions, and the very real impact of cultural differences on leading for peak performance.

As shown in the diagram below, a leader is in a unique position, in relationships with many people making demands on their time within the context of the organization. Outside of the organization are demands created by competitors, legislation, stakeholders, technology, and the economic conditions as a whole. These interrelationships create opportunities but also challenges. The leader must have an effective system for managing the demands and requirements of the boss, peers, direct reports, and clients, while at the same time providing motivational leadership. The FACTS approach has a role to play in all of these interactions.

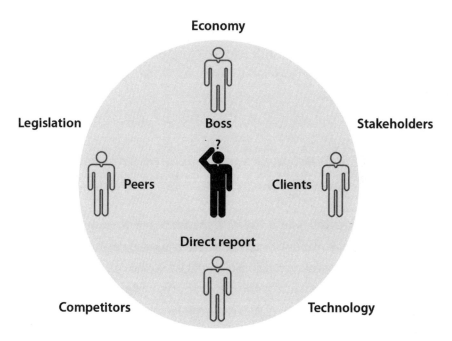

The player-coach challenge

However, before we dive into that, we need first to address the "elephant in the room." We have delivered a number of "leader as coach" workshops to international business leaders and have found varying levels of engagement. There are leaders who immediately get the coaching concept, there are healthy skeptics who wait to be convinced, and then there are leaders who believe that this is nothing to do with them. When discussing pure coaching, the objections that are typically voiced include:

- ❑ "I haven't got the time."
- ❑ "I don't believe in my people."
- ❑ "My bonus is not linked to developing people."
- ❑ "Where would I start—my team, my boss, my clients?"
- ❑ "I don't have a team."
- ❑ "I haven't got the confidence/skills to do this."
- ❑ "Isn't this different depending on national culture?"
- ❑ "It won't work."
- ❑ "Even if I believed in this, my company culture will not support it."
- ❑ "How do I do this in an open-plan office, remotely, or in 15 minutes on the phone?"

When digging underneath these objections, we often find a belief that "my job is to deliver business results, not develop people." Often leaders are recruited to drive performance through a business, to deliver financial results and maximize return on investment. These are hard, "macho," task-oriented activities, far removed from the softer skills of developing people and nurturing talent, and certainly a long way from the notion of person-centered coaching. Also consider a typical career progression.

Young people are initially appointed into a "doing" role because of their technical ability and their success then leads to career progression into supervisory, managerial, and leadership roles. The technical expertise that originally attracted them into a profession is no longer so important; planning, strategy, and coordinating become more appropriate. The "doers" become "managers," as represented in the diagram below, a transition that some leaders welcome but is resisted by others. Holding on to the desire to "do" precludes having the space and time to manage, plan for the future, and create strategies, all of which are essential for sustainable business growth.

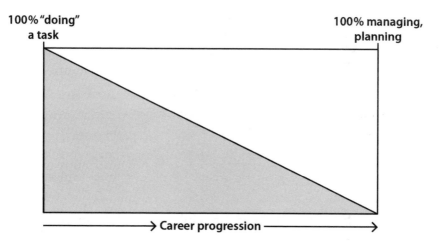

A transition to 100 percent manager is not practical or desirable. Consider a sporting metaphor: the "doers" are the players of the field, they are part of the team working up a sweat and willing to give everything to score a point or a goal. Then take the role of a sporting coach, sat on the sidelines during the game, responsible for building the best team, developing the skills of individuals, and determining the strategy for each game. Moving away from the direct contact of the game to become a coach is often too much in one leap; in a similar way, when business professionals are promoted they sometimes struggle to know whether to stay as a "player" or become a "hands-off" manager. However, there is an alternative: a player-coach who is on the field interacting with the other players, in direct contact with the opposition while still managing others. In this hybrid role the player-coach is also planning the strategy for the game and developing the team. Successful soccer player-coaches include Kenny Dalglish at Liverpool, Ruud Gullit at Chelsea, and Gregg Berhalter at Los Angeles Galaxy. This is an approach that is understandable and accessible for many business leaders, allowing the leader to apply the FACTS principles in 10–20-minute focused bursts as an integrated element of their day-to-day business activities.

In demanding times, many leaders struggle with the notion of traditional coaching, as the greatest need is to focus on business performance and drive hard for results. There is a tendency to revert to a style that pushes harder and drives faster, to "tell and do," and abandon developing people through a coaching approach; this is simply a luxury that time and pressure do not allow. The player-coach enables challenge and support to happen simultaneously, so why be a player or a coach when you can be both?

Where are you currently on the 100 percent player to 100 percent coach continuum? There is no right or wrong answer, as each role is different and each company has a unique approach.

↑ **100% player**

↓ **100% coach**

Think what it could be like if you moved 10 percent more toward the coaching end of the spectrum. What would you be doing differently, what would the team be doing differently, what are the implications, what are the possible advantages to you, the team, and the organization?

We are not asking leaders to move lock, stock, and barrel to the coaching end. This is not practical or desirable. We are not slaves to coaching, we are not "coaching fundamentalists," but we do know the benefits of coaching in business. We would challenge each leader to make a 10 percent move toward the coaching end of the scale, to experiment with a new approach, and to evaluate the change (we are still in the laboratory of learning). This is about being bold, taking a risk, and trying something new. Success breeds success, a small win creates the confidence to commit to the next step, and so a 10 percent move can then lead to a 20 percent move toward the coaching end. There is a right balance on the player–coach spectrum for each person, but to find this balance you must test out alternatives and decide on the correct approach for you. If you are willing to accept this challenge, then plan, experience, evaluate—and do it again.

FACTS in management practice

Now we have set the challenge, we will turn to practical situations that leaders face and suggest how the FACTS model can be used to achieve peak performance. The FACTS approach linked with the principles we set out earlier are crucial in any leadership position. As a reminder, these principles are:

❑ Passionate curiosity
❑ Trust in the future potential of all

- ❏ Letting go of status, expertise, and outcomes
- ❏ Speak your truth and face the FACTS
- ❏ Build the contract and honor the contract

Taking each of these in turn from a purely business leadership perspective, we will describe what we mean:

- ❏ *Passionately curious*—"As a leader I want to find answers, to solve business problems, to understand customer needs and stakeholder expectations."
- ❏ *Trust in the future potential of all*—"As a leader I believe that I and the team within this organization can achieve the goals we have set out. I also believe that our customers have the potential to grow with us and that new markets will emerge."
- ❏ *Letting go of status, expertise, and outcomes*—"As a leader I no longer need to be a technical expert, I have good people around me to do this, I am now an expert in process, coordination, problem solving, motivation, and managing relationships. I will achieve my goals through my team."
- ❏ *Speak your truth, face the FACTS*—"As a leader I will be authentic, genuine, and consistent, I will face the truth, will not hide away from difficult situations, and will achieve a positive outcome."
- ❏ *Build the contract, honor the contract*—"As a leader I will make it clear to my direct reports, my peers, and my boss what they can expect from me and what I expect from them. I will establish a consistent and clear approach for working with customers and suppliers that delivers what I have agreed."

In applying the FACTS approach we will consider delegation, performance management, personal objective setting, and effective communication with boss, peers, team members, and clients.

Delegation

One way for a leader to move toward the coach end of the player–coach spectrum is by creating time and space. However, time is finite and cannot be conjured up by some form of business alchemy. Delegation is a practical way to free up time and allow more for strategic planning and preparation. Consider the dialogue below:

LEADER: Jane, can I see you for 30 minutes at 2 pm please? There's a piece of work I'd like you to do...

LEADER: [Later] Jane, thanks for coming along. As I mentioned, I'd like you to do this piece of work. We need to research the oil market and make an investment recommendation for the board meeting next Friday. Can you do this? (*courageous goal*)

DIRECT REPORT: I've never done a board report before, that sounds a bit scary. (*speak your truth*)

LEADER: I know you're the best person for the job, you have the greatest knowledge of the oil market, and the analysis report you produced last month for me was excellent. We can have regular meetings to review how you're progressing. (*trust in the future potential of all*)

DIRECT REPORT: OK, but let me clarify a few things first. When you say the oil market, do you mean current consumption levels across the globe along with forecasts? (*build the contract*)

LEADER: Yes, current usage, with forecast.

DIRECT REPORT: OK, what format do you want the report to be in? (*build the contract*)

LEADER: Here's a copy of my last board paper that you can use as a template.

DIRECT REPORT: In terms of length, what have you got in mind? (*build the contract*)

LEADER: No more than 2500 words.

DIRECT REPORT: And to help me put this into context, how will the board use this information, and what do you see happening following the meeting? (*systems thinking*)

LEADER: Good question. The board is looking at the long-term investment portfolio and Henderson's, the external advisers, have proposed oil as a growth market, but I want to check it out independently so the board has a balanced view. So what other information do you need?

DIRECT REPORT: That's helpful, I'm clear. But I have to say this will take up all of my time, so I won't be able to work on the zoning project. (*speak your truth*)

LEADER: I understand. The board report is higher priority, the zoning project can be pushed back a few days, and I'll talk to Dave about this. OK, let's agree a 30-minute review meeting on Tuesday afternoon and again on Thursday morning. If you're OK with that, talk me through your initial ideas for how you might do this, the stages you have in mind, and who you might talk to. (*systems thinking, feedback*)

The key to successful delegation is preparation and effective communication. The leader asked Jane for a meeting at 2 pm and so had time to plan the delegation. Consider the lifecycle of our FACTS approach and how this maps onto the process of delegation.

Build the contact, honor the contract
This is the crucial first step, to build an understanding of what must be done, how the task will be undertaken, agree who will

do what (your role as a leader, their role, and that of other people), what support is needed, and what resources are required, as well as monitoring progress and checking the processes agreed. There is a saying "Delegate the task, not the process," which means clearly identifying what must be done, and detailing an unambiguous end point relating to quality, quantity, and deadline. Once this is done, check that you both share the same understanding of what needs to be done, and then allow the person to determine their own route for delivery; they own the process to achieve the end point.

Speak your truth, face the FACTS

The delegation process requires openness, an adult-to-adult conversation. We can think of many examples of when delegation did not work because there was no clarity on the end point. Understanding must be checked and the truth spoken so that the person who has been delegated to is free to question openly— "What is the purpose of the task?" "How will this be used?" "How will this contribute to the organization's success?" "If I focus my attention on this task, how will it affect my bonus?" We may be familiar with junior people accepting a delegated task because they felt they had to as they could not say no to a more senior person, and the task is not completed because the junior person is overloaded. It is the leader's responsibility to create an environment where it is acceptable and encouraged to face the facts and speak the truth.

Feedback

The milestones for the achievement of the overall task are monitored and feedback provided to ensure that achievement. As always, feedback should be honest and include praise as recognition of effective work, as well as challenge for work that is not up to the agreed standard.

Accountability

The achievement of the task is delegated and with this responsibility and accountability are also delegated. The person is held accountable for the action they have agreed to undertake so that quality standards and timescales are achieved. Also, the leader is held accountable for the provision of resources and support.

Courageous goals

The goal agreed in the contract stage is exciting and motivational, so that the individual is committed to and passionate about achieving the delegated task.

Tension

Tension is built to an optimal level for the person receiving the delegation. This is done through milestone meetings and feedback.

Systems thinking

There is confidence that achievement of the milestones will help the achievement of the overall task and this in turn will contribute to the organizational goals and the needs of wider stakeholders. Long-term effects are understood and the consequences known.

Managing performance

Managing performance is the amalgamation of a number of activities to ensure that levels of effective performance are maintained. This is often associated with managing the poor performance of an individual. A model for performance that we use frequently is:

Performance = understanding x capability x motivation

For performance to be high, the individual needs to understand what is required, the end product, the quality standard, and the timescale. Once there is this clear understanding, the person needs the basic skills so that they are capable of achieving the required outcome. The final factor of motivation is the most important but is often intangible, as this is an internal factor only known by the individual themselves: do they want to do the task at hand, are they excited and engaged? As the factors in this formula are multiplied together, as with any numerical formula of this sort, if one factor is zero, then the end product is also zero, so it is important that each factor is in place and has a positive value. It is the leader's responsibility to create the conditions to ensure that peak performance is achieved.

We all know of people whose performance has not been up to the right standard and eventually the organization and the person went their separate ways. This can be painful for the individual, line manager, and organization, as well as a time-consuming and costly process. This can happen even when delegation is as effective as possible. Avoiding this damaging situation in the first place is good, but achieving a positive result out of a negative situation is even better. That is why effective performance management is an investment worth making. If a company has spent a lot of time and money hiring and developing an individual, they are an asset of value, but they also have hidden value in terms of latent potential. So if the work performance of an individual dips, the leader has a clear role in working with that person to bring the "asset" back on stream.

Consider the role of FACTS in this process using the diagram overleaf as an illustration. This shows a line of performance over time for one person; you can see that performance is at a constant level and then falls off. At this point the leader has a meeting with the individual concerned.

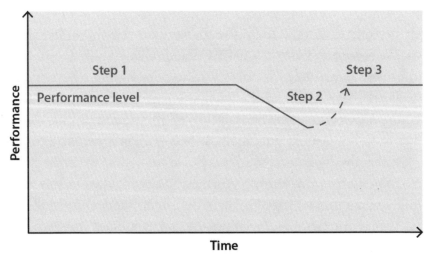

Consider the following dialogue (with FACTS principles and skills in italics):

> LEADER: Donna, thanks for coming to see me. We agreed an hour for this meeting, is this still OK for you? (*build the contract*)
>
> DIRECT REPORT: Yes, that's fine, but I must make a phone call to a client at 4 pm.
>
> LEADER: That will be fine. Donna, I wanted to see how things are with you at the moment. I've noticed that some of your work has not been up to its usual standard. The report on the Murray contract was a day late and there were two errors in it, and also I had an email from Murray's saying that they were unhappy with the level of service they were getting. (*speak your truth, feedback*)
>
> DIRECT REPORT: What specifically did the email say?
>
> LEADER: It was from Janet, our main contact, and she said that she had to chase you three times for cost information last month, and when she received it she had to spend a day reformatting it. This feedback came as a surprise to me, and then linked with what I have

noticed myself, this just doesn't seem to be what I've seen of you in the past. What are your thoughts on this? (*feedback*)

DIRECT REPORT: Yes, sorry, it's not good enough. I'll focus more on this in the future.

LEADER: Donna, what's behind this? (*passionate curiosity, tension*)

DIRECT REPORT: Nothing, all is good. Now I really need to make that phone call.

LEADER: You have plenty of time. I feel that there is something that remains to be discussed, and you seem to be holding back. What is it? (*passionate curiosity, speak your truth, tension*)

DIRECT REPORT: OK, to tell you the truth I'm bored with the Murray work. I've been doing it for 18 months now and it never changes, it's the same reports, nothing is new. I feel like I'm in a rut and I'm not progressing.

LEADER: I did not know you felt like this, tell me more. I genuinely want to know so we can resolve this matter. (*passionate curiosity*)

DIRECT REPORT: As you know, I've been doing some additional work for Sue that's much more interesting. This is cutting-edge stuff and really plays to my strengths. I want to focus more on that. And I guess I've taken my eye off the ball with the Murray work because I've lost interest. (*speak your truth*)

LEADER: I'm beginning to understand. But we still have the Murray work to do and you're the project manager; you're accountable for this. You need to manage this, not just drop it. (*accountability and tension*)

DIRECT REPORT: This isn't what I signed up for. When you took me on you talked about the opportunity to develop and take on a variety of challenging work. This hasn't happened. I just feel like a robot here to churn the numbers. I want more and that's what we agreed when I joined. (*speak your truth, feedback, honor the contract*)

LEADER: This is clearly a big issue, and more complex than I originally anticipated. What do you propose we do?

DIRECT REPORT: I don't want to do the Murray work, and I want to look at the higher-level contracts like the one I'm working on with Sue. (*speak your truth*)

LEADER: I understand what you say, and it's good to have such an open conversation. We should have done this some time ago; I'm sorry we didn't. We should reflect on this. I'll think about what can be done so that you're involved in the higher-level deals, and also talk to Sue. But I want you to come up with a plan for how we can repair the relationship with Murray's, and if you want to delegate this to someone else I'd like your recommendation for who this will be and a detailed hand-over plan. (*build the contract, accountability*)

DIRECT REPORT: That sounds fair.

LEADER: If you're free on Monday at 10 am we can get back together for an hour to discuss this further in some detail.

This dialogue has uncovered a motivational issue and followed a three-step process to reach resolution.

Step 1: Build the contact, honour the contract

This step is all about building the understanding in our performance equation. As with delegation, this ensures that the person knows what to do, to what standard, and by when. The leader also checks understanding by asking questions for clarification, asking the person to repeat back their understanding, and so on. If this step is done thoroughly, there is a high probability of achieving a successful outcome.

Step 2: Speak your truth, face the FACTS

Performance begins to drop off, possibly a milestone is not achieved on time, errors are present, a client complains, or a contract is lost. This is the place for facing the facts, and speaking the truth through clear and concrete feedback. In practice many leaders avoid this sort of discussion: they hope the problem corrects itself; they think the individual is a professional and should be able to do it for themselves; or the leader is simply too busy. However, this is not realistic: the problem doesn't go away or correct itself and the potential damage to the reputation of the company or impact on the morale of other members of staff is immeasurable. This matter must be resolved quickly through a courageous conversation that will go into the zone of uncomfortable debate; tension will rise, potentially to a level that the leader will find uncomfortable. Nevertheless, the elephant is in the room and has to be dealt with.

There is an upside, as a conversation will lead to a breakthrough when performance levels improve and actually exceed initial levels, or the person clearly understands that they are not in the right role. With a positive vision, the leader provides feedback on what actually happened (observation) and its impact: what are the beliefs or assumptions the leader or other stakeholders hold based on what has happened? The leader does this with a view to understanding what has happened and why, and so the leader is passionately curious. There is no blame or accusation, this is two adults discussing an issue, seeking understanding. The leader will do this to determine which factor in the performance equation is missing: has the individual not understood, is there a skill gap and they are not capable, or is it that they are not motivated? The leader then invites input and listens.

Step 3: Accountability and action

Action can be taken once the elephant in the room has been dealt with. In this step the contract is rebuilt, responsibility is allocated, and agreed action taken to increase the levels of understanding, capability, or motivation. Milestones are established, commitments made, and accountability determined. A key stage here is an understanding of consequences: what are the consequences if the contract is broken after this agreement has been made?

Through this three-stage process performance is managed, maintained, and enhanced, while a solid foundation is established for the future.

Personal objective setting

Personal objective setting is a crucial part of any organization and is frequently seen in appraisal processes and personal development plans, often linked to bonus payments. This direct link to pay certainly focuses the attention and drives performance. However, it can also produce some unexpected outcomes.

If you consider a person-centered approach to objective setting, the leader would ask their direct reports "What objectives will you set yourself for this year?"—this is a great nondirective stance to start from and will allow the individual to identify what is really important to them and be motivated through ownership of the goal. This extreme devolution may not happen to this extent in practice, but a number of training programs for leaders suggest this approach. The link to pay may mean that the individual wants to ensure that the bonus payment is maximized and the risk of failure minimized. To do this the objective is scaled back, and an easily achievable goal is set. You may ask: "How can you be so cynical and distrusting?" We have seen this in practice and it's a long way from the courageous goals we spoke about in Chapter 6. Where is the excitement, risk, or audacity of a goal that is knowingly achievable to ensure the payment of a bonus?

So if a leader wants to ensure that the employee owns the goal and wants to achieve it, what can they do? The answer comes from our favorite word, "challenge." For example, at the annual appraisal meeting the leader and a direct report have the following discussion (with FACTS principles and skills in italics):

LEADER: What objectives do you want to set for yourself this year? (*build the contract*)

DIRECT REPORT: A 5 percent increase in revenue and margin.

LEADER: That's an admirable objective, but it sounds safe. I'm sure you can achieve more. What else can you give me? (*tension and courageous goals*)

DIRECT REPORT: This will be a push given the market and the competition, but I guess I could increase it to 6 percent.

LEADER: You know that as a business we're looking for an overall increase of 10 percent, and as your part of the business is the most profitable, you'll be expected to deliver a higher rate. (*systems thinking*)

DIRECT REPORT: I understand the organizational context, but given the resources available it's a stretch.

LEADER: If your bonus was guaranteed for the next 12 months and not at risk and you were being the bravest you could possibly be, what would your target be? (*tension and courageous goals*)

DIRECT REPORT: To be honest, 15 percent.

LEADER: OK, given your performance last year I think you can do more and our shareholders will be expecting more, so what else would really excite you? (*feedback, tension, courageous goals, and systems thinking*)

DIRECT REPORT: That's a stretch; I can't go further than that.

LEADER: Look at your numbers this year; I'm confident you can. Forget the percentages, what would really excite you? (*tension and courageous goals*)

DIRECT REPORT: To bring in the next big trophy client.

LEADER: Now, that sounds exciting. If you did that, what would the value be? (*courageous goals*)

DIRECT REPORT: If it was on the same scale as Brookes, it would increase our revenue by 20 percent with a healthy margin, but I will need more support.

LEADER: If you focus your attention on this, what will be the knock-on long-term effect? (*systems thinking*)

DIRECT REPORT: I won't be able to provide the level of support I've been offering to some of the smaller accounts and we'll need to look at the contracts to ensure that everything is within scope or is paid for additionally. Someone else will need to do this.

LEADER: I understand what you say and this sounds a target that I would be excited about and it will focus my attention. I also hear what you say about resources, so let's agree that your objective will be to bring in the next trophy client in 12 months and you can come back by the end of next week with a business case for the resources you need. Are you up for that? (*accountability*)

DIRECT REPORT: Yes.

LEADER: I'll put a date in the diary for the end of next week to review and discuss how this can be achieved. (*accountability*)

In this dialogue the leader is open to entering the zone of uncomfortable debate if necessary and to pushing and stretching, considering a systems thinking perspective of what the organization requires given the demands of shareholders and also the wider implications for existing clients. The leader challenges the direct report five times in this short dialogue and achieves a motivational objective, whereas other leaders may have accepted a lower figure. A crucial point is that this is not a bullying boss pressurizing a junior person into accepting unrealistic objectives. The leader believes in the potential of this individual and is aware of their capability and so is confident in their ability to deliver. This is an intervention that the leader planned and prepared for in advance to increase the tension to an optimal level for this person. The leader will take a different approach for a different individual based on calibrating each person's response to challenge over time. The leader has a repertoire of skillful interventions to deploy given each unique situation.

Managing upward

Our fourth example of applying FACTS is the common situation of managing upward and using FACTS to influence the boss. In our previous example we looked at the personal objective-setting process. Now we will look at this from the perspective of the direct report applying these skills in the annual appraisal meeting with their boss. Consider the following dialogue:

LEADER: This is the time of year to review objectives and see how you've done against the targets we set last April.

DIRECT REPORT: I'm glad we're having this talk, especially as the mid-term review meeting did not take place. You'll remember I booked a meeting twice but they were both canceled. I was beginning to think this was not a serious process and you were interested in other things. (*feedback, speak your truth and face the facts*)

LEADER: Yes, good point, my diary has been a bit hectic, especially with the integration following the acquisition. I'm sorry you got that impression; it wasn't my intention. This is an important process, but I guess other things have been important as well.

DIRECT REPORT: I understand. We've all been incredibly busy. If I agree to do something for you, I make sure I do, and I would hope that you can do the same.

LEADER: Point taken. I can't promise not to cancel meetings in the future, but if I do, I'll reinstate and commit not to cancel a second time. (*build the contract, honor the contract*)

LEADER: Now let's take look at your objectives. I notice that you delivered £100,000 against the target of £150,000 for new business. This is disappointing given your numbers last year.

DIRECT REPORT: Yes, I can see that there's a shortfall. I'm disappointed about this too. You will remember that I was off line for three months sorting out the issues with client contracts relating to the integration. That was a significant input that ensured that the integration was seamless from our client's perspective. Post-integration we have retained 95 percent of clients, and we estimated we would only retain 80 percent. I couldn't have done both. (*speak your truth and feedback*)

LEADER: But I expected £150,000.

DIRECT REPORT: Given the significance of retaining clients, I took the decision to focus my attention in that area, not to be distracted by generating new business. Given the long-term value of retaining existing clients, I'm confident that it was the right decision. (*systems thinking and tension*)

LEADER: I can understand what you're saying. When I was preparing for this meeting, I was going to assess your performance as "C"; however, I can understand that would be harsh given the reality of your activity over the year, and the value of retaining the existing clients. Based on this, I'll assess you as "B."

In this scenario the original contract relating to the mid-term review meetings had been broken; the boss had canceled the meeting twice and so devalued the perceived importance of the appraisal process and damaged the trust in the relationship. The reportee has faced this truth and provided feedback. In a tense and difficult conversation, the reportee has consistently spoken the truth from a factual and unemotional position that cannot be denied. In taking action, the reportee considered the wider systems thinking perspective, rather than the narrow person-centered view that would maximize their personal bonus. By focusing on the bigger picture of retaining existing clients, the reportee has added significant value on a long-term basis to the business. By speaking the truth, providing feedback, and being comfortable using tension and working in the zone of uncomfortable debate, the reportee has changed the boss's opinion. A win/win position is achieved: maximizing business benefit, maximizing personal bonus payment, and rebuilding the trust in the relationship.

Client negotiation

Our fifth example of applying FACTS relates to client interaction, a crucial and unavoidable business process that can make or break the success of a business and personal earnings when profitability is linked to bonus. There are customer service mantras that say "the customer is king" and "the customer is always right," but more recently these have been questioned. The customer is not always right; the very nature of the interaction makes the supplier the expert. The customer may not know what they need or want, or know the best solution for the business. Also, what the customer wants may not make good business for a supplier. Every customer would want the highest quality at the lowest price, but from a supplier's perspective there is no economic margin in a transaction based on providing a Rolls-Royce for the price of a Nissan Micra.

In FACTS terms this is about building a contract that is honored through speaking the truth, providing feedback, being comfortable with tension and the zone of uncomfortable debate as needed, and taking a systems thinking approach. If a supplier says "yes" to everything a customer wants, there is the risk that a contract is built that cannot be honored. Consider the following dialogue:

> SUPPLIER: We are 12 months into this five-year contract and this is a good time to review and take stock. I would welcome your feedback. (*feedback*)
> CUSTOMER: This is a big contract and after an initial honeymoon period we had a few problems that you

are aware of. However, that has settled down now and we are pleased with the service over the last four months.

SUPPLIER: What has pleased you particularly? (*feedback*)

CUSTOMER: Your account management team are now very fast at responding to our requests for information. Previously it would take them up to a week to respond; now it's a matter of hours. I definitely feel that you're now adding value to our business.

SUPPLIER: I'm pleased that things are better now. Given the length of this contract, we certainly want things to get off to a good start and work in partnership with you. (*build the contract*)

CUSTOMER: Partnership is a good word.

SUPPLIER: I'm glad you mentioned the requests for additional information, as this is something I want to talk about. I acknowledge there were some teething problems, which we addressed and put right. Aware of this, the account management team were very keen to do everything to help you. However the requests for additional information have increased over time, initially from one a month in the first two months to ten a month in the last four months. You will remember the amount of time you and I spent on the contract and when we signed it we were certain that it was right and covered everything. Unfortunately, with these requests for additional information the scope of the contract has expanded. What is your take on this? (*feedback, speak your truth, accountability*)

CUSTOMER: Yes, it became clear that this additional information was very useful and gave us valuable real-time data and we would like this to continue.

SUPPLIER: I'm pleased that we're able to add value. You will remember that the contract mentioned that work out of scope is chargeable, and given the level of work I want to discuss the charges with you. (*build the contract, honor the contract, ZOUD*)

CUSTOMER: This was not what I was expecting, and I don't have funds available for extra fees.

SUPPLIER: I understand this is a surprise, but it's an important area to talk through face to face. I've calculated that the additional work is taking up half a day a week above the normal contracted work, which is clearly a significant amount. (*tension, speak your truth*)

CUSTOMER: I don't have any additional funds.

SUPPLIER: I hear what you say, but we entered into this relationship with a clearly defined contract. You and I spent weeks getting the contract right; now it's time to put all that effort into play. (*tension, build the contract, ZOUD*)

CUSTOMER: I remember the effort to get the contract right, but I expect you to do the extra work as a gesture of goodwill, given the size and duration of this deal.

SUPPLIER: That's what we have been doing for the last four months. It's time either to stop this additional work or, if the information is adding value to your business, we will charge for it as agreed in the contract. (*tension, ZOUD*)

CUSTOMER: I can see this is an important issue to you and you're not going to back down. This partnership has worked well up to now, and yes, the additional work has been valuable. OK, I will pay from 1 April onward. However, I want a detailed breakdown of the additional work, with time spent, and you and I will sit down to review this every six months.

The cultural perspective

In reviewing each of these examples and dialogues, we are conscious that they are written from a predominantly Anglo-Saxon perspective. It is true that applying the FACTS approach either as a coach or a leader will be dependent on the organizational and country culture in which it is being done. Each culture will have its own norm on the support/challenge axis, with some being more naturally comfortable with a more challenging approach and others more sensitive to this style.

One of the most famous studies of cross-cultural differences is the research of Professor Geert Hofstede, which was conducted across 72 countries within IBM in the early 1970s and published as *Culture's Consequences*. Hofstede developed a "4D" model in which he catalogued each culture according to the following dimensions:

❑ *Power distance*—the extent to which the less powerful members of institutions accept that power is distributed unequally.
❑ *Individualism*—the extent to which people are expected to look after themselves and their immediate family only.
❑ *Masculinity*—the extent to which the dominant values in a society are achievement and success, as opposed to caring for others and quality of life.
❑ *Uncertainty avoidance*—the extent to which people feel threatened by ambiguous situations and try to avoid them.

Hofstede plotted each country across these dimensions, noting the extremes in the table overleaf.

	Power distance	Individualism	Masculinity	Uncertainty avoidance
High	Malaysia	USA	Japan	Greece
Medium	France	Portugal	Belgium	Canada
Low	Austria	Guatemala	Sweden	Singapore

Relating Hofstede's work to the FACTS approach suggests that FACTS would be most natural to those cultures where power distance is low, individualism is high, masculinity is high, and uncertainty avoidance is low. The country cultures that most closely fit this profile are Canada, Ireland, New Zealand, Switzerland, the UK, and the USA. In contrast, examples of countries with the opposite profile are France, Greece, Portugal, Turkey, and Uruguay.

Of course, any such generalizations are coarse and simplistic, since within each country are many diverse company cultures and many diverse individuals. However, this brief foray into the world of cross-cultural management does highlight that applying any model such as FACTS is sensitive to the context in which it is applied, hence our examples and dialogues need to be interpreted carefully to take account of this factor. It is not within the scope of this book to explore the cross-cultural factor in any depth, although we recognize the need for further research and understanding in this area.

Applying the FACTS approach

In this chapter we have presented leaders with practical applications of FACTS relating to delegation, performance management, personal objective setting, managing upward, client interaction, and the impact of cultural differences. Each of these examples is different and requires a different emphasis on certain parts of the model. All elements of the FACTS model and its principles are applicable to each business situation; however, a skilled leader will have a detailed understanding of FACTS and apply the components to a varying degree to achieve the desired outcome.

FACTS is not a sequential model to be slavishly followed, but an iterative and flexible process. The approach has much to offer leaders who want to drive business results and develop people. These are not mutually exclusive, in that business results are achieved *or* people developed and motivated; through the application of FACTS, both are possible in a symbiotic relationship. In fact, challenging coaching is a mechanism for engaging and motivating individuals and teams to develop self-sufficiency and sustained levels of high performance at a systems-centered and organizational level. As leaders ourselves, we have seen this in practice and can speak from experience.

EXERCISE

- ❑ If you moved by 10 percent to the coach end of the player–coach continuum, what would you be doing differently?
- ❑ Take a risk—do it!

CHAPTER 10

The deeper FACTS

Though some say it is useless to accept responsibility for the calamities and toxicities of the world, taking such responsibility might put us on the road to the Way. (Tao Te Ching, Verse 78)

In this chapter we lift our sights to look beyond immediate, practical applications of the FACTS approach in the business world to explore deeper, broader questions regarding the relevance of this model to future trends in society at large. In so doing we shift from the language of support and challenge to that of freedom and responsibility. These words may provoke you into thinking that we are about to make ideological or even political points. This is not our intention; we remain focused on behaviors not "-ologies," an angle that we explore further at the end of the chapter. We will also refer to and expand the model of "dependence/independence/interdependence" that is covered in more detail in other texts.

The freedom/responsibility matrix

We have highlighted the risks of the "me, me, me" style of coaching and throughout this book we have encouraged coaches to adopt a more challenging stance by using FACTS. In this approach individuals are expected to take greater responsibility for the impact of their actions on others in the wider organizational system.

In the same way as we suggested that the optimum conditions for performance come from finding the right balance between support and challenge, in this chapter we extend this premise to suggest that the optimal conditions for performance come from finding the right balance between seeking personal freedom and taking responsibility for the collective good. This parallel is shown in the diagram below:

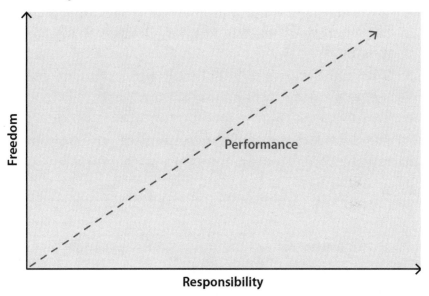

This chart suggest that as you challenge others more, you are asking them to take greater responsibility for the consequences of their actions on themselves and on others. Similarly, when you are supporting others and helping them raise their self-awareness, you are giving them a greater sense of personal freedom. Traditional coaching approaches have tended to promote personal freedom, whereas the FACTS coaching approach shifts the emphasis to promote greater levels of personal responsibility.

As far as we know there is no empirical evidence to support the correlation between freedom and responsibility. It is an intuitive leap, yet is a potentially powerful idea that we will explore further from an experiential perspective. The idea of linking freedom and responsibility in this way raises the following questions:

- ❑ What four quadrants in the freedom/responsibility matrix are the equivalents of those we developed earlier for support/ challenge?
- ❑ What are the wider business and societal trends regarding freedom and responsibility?
- ❑ What new light might this connection shed on leadership and coaching approaches and the relevance of the FACTS mindset?
- ❑ What is the "bigger picture" here in which coaching and the business world may be playing a crucial role?

To create a freedom/responsibility matrix we can create quadrants that represent the following stances in a coaching relationship:

H

	Independence	Interdependence
Freedom	Dependence	Co-dependence

L **Responsibility** H

These quadrants describe the nature of the relationship between coach and coachee. They represent the shifting balance that exists as freedom and responsibility wax and wane. To have freedom is to gain power in a relationship, so these stances could also be regarded as mapping the balance of power at any point in time. Both parties establish and review an agreement about how power will be exercised in the relationship and this plays out in terms of the relative freedom and responsibility that each party secures.

As we noted earlier, often this psychological contract is unwritten and subconscious, but nevertheless its existence is clear to external observers. Is one party willing to give up power and, if so, in return for what? Is one party willing to assume power and, if so, in return for what? The quadrants represent different psychological contracts that are built and maintained between individuals and within teams and organizations. We have labeled the quadrants according to the type of dependency that exists in the relationship.

Low responsibility/low freedom

We term this the dependent state: a situation where the relationship between two individuals involves one party abdicating responsibility to the other and in exchange losing a degree of personal freedom. It is the culture of a command-and-control organization and a totalitarian political regime. It is the natural state of a young child who is dependent on parental figures, has little freedom, and relies on them to take responsibility. Using Maslow's hierarchy of needs, this type of relationship is driven by the need of the dependent party to belong and the need for the other party to establish their self-esteem and status.

Low responsibility/high freedom

We term this the independent state: a situation where one party has claimed a measure of personal freedom but is still expecting the other party to take responsibility for the wider consequences of their actions. Some will immediately recognize a teenage son or daughter who may reside in this quadrant! Yet it is not a state exclusive to those who are adolescent in age; it is also inhabited by those adults and organizations who are psychologically adolescent in their relationships with others. Using Maslow's hierarchy of needs, both parties in this quadrant are focused on and driven by their respective status and self-esteem needs.

High responsibility/low freedom

We term this the co-dependent state: a situation where individuals take excessive responsibility for the consequences of other people's behavior. In so doing they give up their own freedom and adopt a "caretaker" role in their relationship with others. They suppress their own needs and become excessively preoccupied with the needs of others. The extreme example of this is the spouse of a violent or addicted partner, who will not choose to end the relationship because they feel responsible for what might happen to the other person and persist in the belief that they can "fix" them. A business example would be a leader whose staff continually breach their legal and psychological contracts but who persists in rescuing them in order to keep the peace. In Maslow's terms, one party sacrifices their needs, whether those be for esteem, safety, or belonging, in order to enable others to remain in a state of denial about the real consequences of their behavior.

High responsibility/high freedom

We term this the interdependent state: a situation in which two parties become genuine partners, sharing responsibility and freedom and maximizing both qualities in each other. This state relies on genuine power sharing in the relationship and assumes that both parties are united in pursuing a common vision via a shared set of values. Both parties collaborate to share their needs and negotiate healthy boundaries. These relationships are ideally observed in functional coalitions where diverse political parties come together to govern a country. In Maslow's terms, both parties move beyond self-esteem and status levels into a focus on self-actualization, which ironically can only be achieved on a collective basis. Self-centered goals are given up in return for a focus on the wider collective good.

The rising tide of freedom

In our earlier discussion of the support/challenge matrix, we noted that the boom times had bred a certain style of coaching that emphasized low challenge/high support skills. In more difficult economic times we suggested that a shift to the high challenge/high support quadrant is healthy, and that this requires different coaching skills to come to the fore. The equivalent statements for the freedom/responsibility matrix would be to suggest that in the boom times the focus was on the attainment of personal freedom and independence, and that in a more demanding environment a shift to the interdependent state will be necessary. Is this true?

To answer this question we need to review the history of freedom and independence in the world at large and in business. Has there been a rise in freedom and independence in recent times? At the "big picture" level, the table overleaf is taken from *Freedom in the World*, an annual comparative assessment of the state of political rights and civil liberties around the globe, published by Freedom House.

In this table, countries are labeled "free," "partially free," or "not free," as measured against detailed checklists that cover topics such as the electoral process, the functioning of government, freedom of expression, and the judicial system.

Year	Free countries	Partly free countries	Not free countries
1976	26%	31%	43%
1986	34%	34%	32%
1996	41%	31%	28%
2006	47%	30%	23%
2007	47%	31%	22%

As the figures show, the conclusion is clear and simple: as economies rise and fall, freedom is on the rise globally. The pace and starting point vary depending on the culture and country concerned, but the trend is clear. There appears to be a universal human drive to seek freedom and to find fulfillment in its achievement. There are many examples from history that support this trend, perhaps the most recent at the time of writing being the unrest in the North African Arab states, which is leading to the relatively peaceful overthrow of dictatorial regimes that have existed for many decades and yet have crumbled almost overnight, as masses of ordinary people choose simultaneously to claim their personal freedom and move beyond a relationship of dependency with regard to their national leaders.

Closer to home, look at those of us in the western developed economies and how free we are compared to our parents. Whether it be the opportunity to be educated and go to university, to become financially independent, to travel, to vote, to get divorced, to follow our sexual or religious preferences, or the freedom technology has brought us, there has been a dramatic leap in levels of freedom in the past generation.

What is the equivalent measure of freedom in the world of business? Possibly the ultimate "freedom cry" in this arena is the decision to be your own boss, to work for yourself. Statistics show that more and more people are having the courage and the opportunity to do this. A generation ago the trend to self-employment would have been biased toward men, but many women are also claiming the freedom not just to work but to work for themselves.

Clearly, the vast majority of the workforce are still in organizations small and large. Yet even here we can see evidence of great leaps in freedom over the past 20 years. More and more people are working from home on a regular basis; a trend partly facilitated by technology, but also reflecting increasing levels of trust in the modern workplace. Recent surveys have demonstrated that flexible working is rated above performance-related bonuses as the most valued employment benefit. And the evidence of the most recent economic crisis has been that unemployment in countries such as the UK has not risen to the levels that were originally forecast. The reason was partly a continuing shift toward freedom inside organizations as workers chose to work fewer hours, take sabbaticals, and retrain rather than lose their job completely. In the downturn, many leading global organizations encouraged their workers either to take unpaid leave or to work a four-day week. People are also taking part-time jobs in greater numbers. For sure, a large proportion of these would prefer to have a full-time job, but a growing minority have the financial freedom to make this choice and more time in their lives for their other interests and commitments.

The development of more freedom in both society and business can be likened to the process of growing up. As children we are born into dependency. We rely on our carers for food, warmth, shelter, and protection. We are needy. In return, we learn to conform to our carers' expectations, we fear their rejection, and we stick within their boundaries of safety. In effect, we give up our power in return for our carers' love and reside in the low responsibility/low freedom quadrant of the freedom/responsibility matrix.

We worship our carers and give them the power of a god in our lives. It works and it is an inevitable stage of our successful development as balanced individuals.

And then comes adolescence... In this period, we rebel against our carers because we suddenly realize that they are not gods and they are not perfect. In fact, in their imperfection, they hurt us as children despite their good intentions. Our ego asserts itself and establishes its independence; we start to experiment with the power this gives us and the ability to satisfy selfish needs. Occasionally, these experiments go wrong and we blame others for our problems. We become independent adults and we walk into the world as free people. We have now migrated to the low responsibility/high freedom quadrant of the matrix.

The transition from dependent toddler to independent adolescent is a natural one. There are those who struggle with this transition and feel threatened by attaining their independence. Then the alternative path is into co-dependency, a situation in which the child does not become a rebellious teenager but opts for a role looking after others and forming relationships where their own needs are compromised in return for a feeling of security and safety. A person in this situation is likely to find that they are quickly in a situation where they are looking after others, whether they be parents, siblings, spouse, or friends.

However, in general as societies and business cultures we are shifting from being dependent toddlers to becoming rebellious teenagers. In the boom times, with the empowering effect of wealth and choice, this trend accelerated, particularly in the western developed economies. In contrast, it could be said that some of the poorer nations exist in a co-dependent state where they sacrifice the needs of their own people to look after the West via the supply of cheap food, resources, and goods. This strays into a political line of thinking that is beyond the focus of this book.

The shift from dependence to independence

Based on this short review, we can sense that in the terms of the freedom/responsibility matrix there is a wholesale shift in society and business from the low freedom/low responsibility quadrant to high freedom/low responsibility, or from dependence to independence.

In *Need, Greed or Freedom,* Sir John Whitmore uses a different language to describe the same transition. He talks of the evolution from inclusion to assertion. He also maps these stages to Maslow's hierarchy of needs, identifying that the inclusion phase is driven by the need to belong and to seek security. The assertion stage is characterized by the quest for status and esteem from others through competing for personal achievements and worldly displays of winning.

We can map the differences between these two stages in terms of their defining motivators and values. The table below summarizes these characteristics.

Dependence	Independence
Focus on belonging and security	Focus on status and achievements
Command and control	Empowerment
Boss/subordinate	Leader/follower
Exploited	Exploiter
Conform	Compete
Powerless	Powerful
"I am safe"	"I am safe and I am free"

As many of us have experienced, the effective way to manage a dependent toddler is very different to what works with a rebellious teenager. When someone is striving for status and achievement rather than belonging and security, they need to be empowered, not controlled. We need to lead them rather than manage them. They shift from being at risk of exploitation to becoming exploiters themselves in their relationships. Out goes the need to conform and in comes the need to compete, in comes power... in comes freedom.

So how do you lead teenagers, free and independent people? Well, it doesn't work to tell them what to do. It particularly doesn't work to tell them what to do if you abused your power over them when they were dependent on you.

For example, it is hard for a priest to preach morality to free adults if he is found to have abused dependent children in his care. It is particularly hard for parents to tell their teenagers what to do if they abused them physically, emotionally, or spiritually. It is particularly hard for leaders to tell their staff what to do if they have previously abused their power and persist in behaving that way toward those who remain dependent on them.

It also doesn't work to give up and stop caring about the people you are responsible for managing or leading. This equates to a parent giving free license to their 14-year-old child to break the law, abuse others including themselves, and generally operate in a boundaryless environment. In business, people are let loose in global, multicultural, high-pressure environments and given challenging targets, then fired when they don't deliver. They rightly question how they were expected to succeed when they felt they were operating in a leadership vacuum: when they did not see their boss from one week to the next and even when they did there was no time for any quality conversation at a personal level. Are these people empowered or are they abandoned?

The first step in the effective leadership of independent people is to accept the reality that they are free and to stop wishing for the return of the "good old days." In other words, it starts with facing the facts. The second step is to think about what style of leadership works for you as a free person. Why would the people who follow you be any different? We suspect it does work for you if your leader makes time to listen to you, to explore your thinking through open questions, and through this to build trust and rapport. It probably works for you when you meet a leader who doesn't insist on subtly knocking your confidence but actually believes that you can do more, be more, blossom, and achieve your dream, without their own ego being threatened by that possibility. It probably suits you when you sense that your leader cares about you and treats you as a unique individual.

We have been fortunate to meet a number of leaders like this in our own careers. We remember each of them with great fondness and respect. We are sure there are those in your career whom you remember likewise. As these relationship-building and influencing skills became more prominent in the business culture of the 1990s, there was a need to create a label for them so that they could be developed, written about, and spoken about more easily. That word became "coaching." In some ways the word worked, because it was clearly not command and control and it was clearly not leaving people totally to their own devices. It was clearly not mentoring and it was clearly not counseling; it was something in the middle. Is it a surprise that in an era where people were seeking freedom, the profession of coaching sprang into being to respond to this need by facilitating the shift from dependence to independence in business cultures?

Traditional person-centered coaching is a perfectly appropriate style of leadership to support people who are in transition from dependence to independence. It reconnects people with their sense of identity and power and it offers a vision of freedom as its goal. In this sense, we are reminded again of the difference between coaching, mentoring, consulting, and therapy. Mentoring rests on a dependence on the mentor's higher expertise and experience in a given area, hence it cannot facilitate a shift to full independence in the mentee without rendering the concept of mentoring itself obsolete. It is a helping tool of the dependent era. This is not a criticism or a slight, simply a recognition of the times in which it appeared and the important yet distinct purpose that it serves.

Consulting rests on a dependence on the consultant's specialist area of expertise. Like mentoring, it is a product of the dependent era, whereby the specialist expertise of the consultant is valued and used to plug gaps in the organization's knowledge and capability. Again, this is a perfectly appropriate means of support in those circumstances.

Therapy is a tool for supporting people who are in a dysfunctional state, often those who have slipped into a co-dependent position and are striving to shift to one of the other three states. Due to the reality of their starting point, therapy has its own unique skills and style in fulfilling the important purpose it has in this overall picture.

However, only the profession of executive coaching can genuinely claim to have been born in the midst of the shift from dependence to independence in business culture. Only coaching is not stigmatized by a history in the dependent world, and only coaching can authentically promote personal freedom and independence without ultimately threatening its own existence. This is not to say that coaching is any better or any worse than the other means of helping people; it simply recognizes that it is different and that its primary audience and purpose may represent a timely intervention in the shifts occurring in the freedom/responsibility matrix over the past generation.

The limits of blind freedom

Nevertheless, within this overall positive trend lies a risk: that we have embraced the goal of freedom without discretion and without limit. We may be in danger of lurching into a phase of "blind freedom" when we worship this value and subordinate all other drives to this one pursuit.

This would be akin to getting stuck as a permanent adolescent, enjoying the crazy parties so much that we resist moving beyond them or growing into the next phase of our development. In popular culture a new term has arisen to capture this phenomenon, the "kidult," which the Urban Dictionary describes as "a so-called grown up who doesn't want to grow up and would instead prefer so-called children's stuff for entertainment." In *Nature and the Human Soul*, Bill Plotkin suggests that as well as a sticking point for individual development, this phenomenon could also be a sticking point for society and culture overall:

> *We live in a largely adolescent world... the majority of humans in developed societies never reach true adulthood ... An adolescent world results in contemporary societies that are materialistic, greed based, hostilely competitive, violent, racist, sexist, ageist and ultimately self destructive. As soon as enough people... progress beyond adolescence the entire consumer driven economy and egocentric lifestyle will implode.*

While Plotkin's diagnosis may seem dramatic and extreme, it is true to say that many of us are so new to freedom that we could be forgiven for desiring freedom as if it were the end in itself rather than the means to a greater end. It is such a novelty, it is like being let loose in the candy shop for the first time with no evil parent to tell you when to stop, so you keep on choosing sweet after sweet and gorging yourself until eventually you get sick! Or like being at a party when you were 17 and you could drink as much as you wanted and you did... and you got sick! It was great fun—to an extent.

Are many of us getting sick on freedom right now? Many of us have found a new toy, a powerful and dangerous toy that we're not used to and that can go to our heads. What are the symptoms of getting sick on freedom? The table below summarizes some of the common symptoms and examples of how they manifest themselves:

Symptoms	Examples
Abuses of power	Rebellion, anger, retribution
Breakdown in trust	Revenge against all authority figures
Denial	"None of this is of my own making"
Lack of responsibility	"I have no impact on anyone or anything outside of myself"
Indulgence	"I want more and I want it now"
Decadence	"I want more and I don't know why"
Unhappiness	"I have everything but I feel nothing"

This is the rallying call of the adolescent western society:

Anyway, this is about me and I don't care about the impact on anyone else. This is my time and my life and I am free to do what I want, thank you very much. What is more, look at all this money I have generated as a result of my freedom. There were some things I never had and now I can have them and this makes me feel really, really good. And when it stopped making me feel really, really good I just carried on having more because I could and no one stopped me. And that also felt good, but for a shorter time. And eventually I got so full of freedom that I couldn't feel anything else any more. I was just totally full and comfortably numb.

Like the character at the end of the Monty Python film *The Meaning of Life*, eventually you find you've had too much of a good thing. You've chosen every item from the menu of the finest restaurant in the world, and now you get the check!

What has this got to with business? A few headline stories from recent years will help answer this question. Remember Nick Leeson, a derivatives broker whose fraudulent, unauthorized, speculative trading caused the collapse of Barings Bank, the UK's oldest investment bank, for which he was sent to prison. His gambling led to total losses of $1.4 billion. As the end loomed, he fled from his office in Singapore leaving a note saying "I'm sorry." However, spin back to the early 1990s and the same Nick Leeson had been lauded as a hero of the financial markets when he made £10 million for Barings, which in that year accounted for 10 percent of its annual profits.

Or take the more recent case of Jérôme Kerviel, a French trader at the bank Société Générale. He was convicted for a breach of trust, forgery, and unauthorized use of the bank's computers, resulting in losses valued at €4.9 billion. Société Générale characterized Kerviel as a rogue trader and claims that he worked these trades alone and without its authorization, assertions that have been met with skepticism from expert commentators and analysts alike. Kerviel, whose is currently pursuing an appeal, told investigators that such practices were widespread and that getting a profit makes the hierarchy turn a blind eye.

The problem with focusing on individuals alone is that it allows us to distance ourselves from such acts and dismiss them as the behavior of crazy people. We don't see them as the tip of a cultural iceberg of our own creation and of our own maintaining. In this way, we let ourselves off the hook; we disconnect and move into judgment of others rather than an assessment of ourselves.

It is easier to see the consequences of this attitude to freedom for the wider culture of an organization via two further examples. The first is Lehman Brothers, the largest bankruptcy in US history that came to be symbolically associated with the global financial crisis. Immediately following the bankruptcy filing, an already distressed financial market began a period of extreme volatility, during which the Dow Jones index experienced its largest one-day point loss, largest intra-day range (more than 1,000 points), and largest daily point gain. What followed was what many have called the perfect storm of economic distress factors and eventually a $700 billion bailout package. Lehman Brothers had exploited the lack of regulation in its markets to lend money to high-risk property purchasers. This act of blind freedom made the bank huge short-term profits but exposed it, and the rest of its stakeholders, to risks that nobody understood or had expressed a desire to be held accountable for. Ultimately, it was the co-dependent US taxpayer who bailed out this recklessness.

Or consider the case of BP and the Deepwater Horizon catastrophe in the Gulf of Mexico. This was the largest accidental marine oil spill in history, killing 11 men and releasing approximately 4.9 million barrels of crude oil into the surrounding ocean. Weeks after the event, and while it was still in progress, the oil spill was being discussed as a disaster with far-reaching consequences that affected global economies and policies. These included structural shifts to energy policy, insurance marketplaces, and risk assessment, and potential liabilities of the order of tens of billions of dollars for several large and well-known companies. It is not the role of this book to examine this example in detail, only to question whether any corporate organization should have had the freedom to take such risks with the environment, the global insurance system, and the lives of its employees. Was this another case of the pursuit of blind freedom at the expense of collective responsibility? Is this what we want?

The shift from independence to interdependence

These examples point to the need for a transition from adolescence to adulthood, from independence to interdependence, from low responsibility/high freedom to high responsibility/high freedom. The value that becomes paramount in facilitating this transition is what a CEO client of ours refers to as the "R" word: *responsibility*. The mere mention of the word is enough to send a shiver down the spine of the western developed world. "Surely there must be an easier way to do this," we cry. "Can't we have our cake and eat it too?" But how is it possible to pursue our own freedom blindly and without limit when we coexist on a planet with restricted resources, limited space, and the inconvenient presence of millions of people with their own unique needs, beliefs, expectations, and desires?

As the famous US lawyer Clarence Darrow once said, "You can only protect your liberties in this world by protecting the other man's freedom. You can only be free if I am free." A similar idea was put in other words by one of the founding fathers of the United States, Thomas Paine, "He that would make his own liberty secure, must guard even his enemy from opposition; for if he violates this duty he establishes a precedent that will reach himself.' This paraphrases what in all the great religions is known as the "golden rule," the simple yet profound invocation to "do unto others as you would have them do unto you."

Using the systems thinking paradigm outlined in Chapter 8, the golden rule is simply a statement about the limits of a system. If everything is connected to everything else, then the moment we step into personal freedom is the moment we also step into personal responsibility. Regardless of the system-level truth of this statement, we can still choose to be in denial of its inevitability. We can outsource our responsibility in at least two ways. We can mortgage the future by claiming our freedom now at the expense of the freedom of others yet to come. A clear example of this would be the freedom to exploit the earth's resources at the expense of their availability for future generations. Second, we can outsource our responsibility to others and, through the strength of our will and the cleverness of our intellect, manipulate these others to accept responsibility for the consequences of our actions. This approach is much more effective if we collude with others to reinforce its impact, which is how the independent, wealthy developed world creates the co-dependent, poverty-stricken developing world.

Regardless of how well we "duck and dive," eventually the system truth catches up with us. Eventually, what is done to others returns to us and we reap what we have sown. Sometimes it may take thousands of years, but the system does not worry about time in the same way we do. It is supremely patient yet supremely just. As with the notion of karma, eventually we meet the consequences of our own actions, eventually we are asked to take responsibility for our own freedom. Using the analogy of a home computer, we are free to download anything we want from the World Wide Web, but if we do this without discretion and care then one stray virus can crash the whole system. Or consider the human body: we are free to hold our breath for as long as we want, but eventually we will fall over. Our freedom has its limits because of the fact that we are a living system in relationship with other living systems. Embracing this reality is the porthole into the interdependent world.

For those who have the stomach for it, the transition from the independent to the interdependent phase involves the shift in behaviors and guiding beliefs summarized in the table below:

Independence	Interdependence
Focus on status and achievements	Focus on meaning and purpose
Empowerment	Coaching
Leader/follower	We/us
Exploiter	Partner
Compete	Collaborate
Powerful	Power sharing
"I am safe and I am free"	"I am safe and I am free and I am responsible"

As we reach the last line of the table, we have to swallow very hard before we can declare the motto of the interdependent age: "I am safe and I am free and I am responsible." This is taking responsibility for the impact of the exercise of our free will on ourselves and on others, on our organization and our wider environment. This is a tall, tall order. Ironically, we feel like we're giving up the very thing we've fought so hard to gain: our freedom. Of course, if we choose responsibility then this is itself an exercise of our free will. There is no sacrifice involved on this basis; we know we are free, we accept this truth, and we choose to put ourselves in service to something bigger than ourselves because we don't need to keep proving our freedom to ourselves and to everybody else on a daily basis. Are we ready for this step?

The link to FACTS coaching

Scanning the characteristics of the interdependent state, we can see the link to the FACTS coaching approach. With its emphasis on challenge rather than support, FACTS is targeted at facilitating the shift from independence to interdependence, from low responsibility/high freedom to high responsibility/high freedom. While empowerment implies granting freedom to those we lead, FACTS coaching tempers this freedom with an emphasis on responsibility, generated through the skills of feedback, accountability, and courageous goal setting in a systems thinking paradigm that knows how to engage and utilize constructive tension. The traditional leader/follower mindset is replaced by the concept of mutual partnerships, in which collaboration rather than competition is the defining principle. As a FACTS coach power is not monopolized, but neither is it given away indiscriminately; there is a mature negotiation that leads to power-sharing agreements for the achievement of specific projects and goals.

Through the shift to the challenging skills of coaching and engaging in the FACTS approach, the coach can promote a sense of personal and collective responsibility. It is clear that a solid foundation of trust and respect must first be built in the relationship. As a coach you must demonstrate repeatedly, and even more so in stressful situations, that you will not snatch away a person's hard-won freedom at the first available opportunity. We must not risk a backward step into a dependent or co-dependent world.

For example, in the midst of a short-term crisis, whether a recession or a lost sales opportunity or a crushing disappointment, there is a temptation for all of us to revert to previous mindsets that create dependency rather than interdependence. Those around you will be acutely sensitive to such moments and they will observe you closely to assess whether you are the real thing or just another actor who, when the chips are down, reverts to self-interest and self-protection. They need to see you tempted by situations involving status and achievement but choosing the path of meaning and purpose; they need to see you given the opportunity to exploit someone and turning away from that; they need to see you power sharing in all areas of your life. They need to see you walk the talk.

Applying this deeper and more philosophical context to the FACTS approach reveals the following connections.

Principles

Build the contract, honor the contract
❏ A clear contract and a high-trust relationship give the coach the opportunity legitimately to introduce "tough love" skills that promote personal and collective responsibility.
❏ The contract is built with the involvement of all major stakeholders and the coach is given permission by these stakeholders to act as the guardian of the contract.
❏ A contract that is broken must lead to consequences for all parties. These are not consequences that the coach administers through a sense of personal power, but rather because it is in the overall interests of the wider organizational system.
❏ Without a contract there are no boundaries. While this maximizes personal freedom, it leads to a "free-for-all" in which

there is no collective purpose, meaning, or feeling of genuine security.

Speak your truth, face the FACTS

❏ When there is transparency of information and honest expression, it becomes difficult for abuses of independence to be perpetuated.

❏ In contrast, when information is hidden and people are intimidated to withhold their opinions, independent/co-dependent relationships can become the "truth that dare not speak its name."

❏ The truth is not intellectually clever, it is intuitively simple. This is why it is accessible to all and not just to those who have a high IQ, monetary wealth, or social fame.

❏ Speaking your truth at the boundary between independence and interdependence is an emotionally charged, volatile, and frightening space. Organizational systems need coaches who have the courage, the training, and the experience to stay centered amid this turmoil.

Approach

Feedback

❏ Feedback is a major tool for exploring the truth of a situation and for highlighting when one person's freedom has compromised that of another, regardless of whether that other person is present or not.

❏ The coach is the voice of all the stakeholders in the system and they are asked to represent these absent stakeholders and give feedback on their behalf in order to avoid systematic abuses of freedom.

❑ Denial is the main mechanism that keeps the era of independence intact. Feedback is one of the main tools that can successfully challenge a state of denial.

Accountability

❑ Personal accountability in the present is what avoids collective guilt in the future. It is what accelerates the transition from independence to interdependence.

❑ Becoming aware of different levels of accountability is what teaches us all to understand that our actions have wider consequences of which we may not be aware.

❑ The coach is the voice of all the stakeholders in the system. They are asked to represent these absent stakeholders and hold accountability on their behalf in order to avoid systematic abuses of freedom.

Courageous goals

❑ The goal of interdependence is potentially the most courageous and exciting goal we can set for ourselves, our organizations, and our society. It is an evolutionary, game-changing milestone that is hard to imagine and feels next to impossible to achieve.

❑ As American cultural anthropologist Margaret Mead famously said, "Never doubt that a small group of thoughtful, committed citizens can change the world. Indeed, it is the only thing that ever has." Hence, individual courageous goals are relevant and important in the context of a collective courageous goal. Where does it start? It always starts with you!

❑ SMART goals are not necessarily transformative because they lack courage. It is very smart to be independent, but it is very courageous to be interdependent.

Tension

❑ There is acute tension at the boundary between independence and interdependence. It is the tension associated with a paradigm shift.

❑ It is very easy to personalize this tension in the coach/coachee relationship, but this is to be mistaken about the bigger picture and make ourselves more important than we really are.

❑ In any transition it is important to optimize the tension. Too little and we will not move from independence to interdependence. Too much and we will get frightened and reach for the dependent and independent comfort zone.

Systems thinking

❑ If everything is connected to everything else, then we can only gain true freedom if others gain their freedom at the same time. Anything less involves us gaining our freedom at the expense of the freedom of someone else and creates a independent/co-dependent relationship, even though the parties may be separated by many miles or many years.

❑ The golden rule is a spiritual teaching that loses its moral dogma and gains a highly practical edge when placed in a systems thinking context. The golden rule is not something that involves us being nice and selfless, but something that involves us being realistic and honest.

❑ The system self-corrects and is morally neutral. The planet does not care if we make the shift from independence to interdependence, in the same way it did not care when the dinosaurs became extinct. Either way, it moves on.

We have covered a great deal of ground in this chapter and its contents may well have left the reader puzzled, confused, and overwhelmed. A book focused on practical coaching skills has launched into a philosophical discussion that touches on global mega-trends. Moreover, the authors have had the temerity to suggest that challenging coaching and the FACTS approach may have a role to play on this grand stage. Who do we think we are?

But the fact is that coaching is the only leadership style that has the potential both to encourage and to respect personal freedom while simultaneously promoting higher levels of personal and collective responsibility. And the fact is that the world of business is uniquely positioned to role model this leadership style on a global scale. Furthermore, there are sustainability challenges that need to be addressed and require a fundamentally new way of relating to both ourselves and our planet. And change can only happen one conversation at a time. These are the FACTS.

At this stage it is tempting to build a complex and compelling "-ology," an empirical model, to add credibility and gravitas to our stance. If we work hard enough at this then we could convince you that these ideas are worth pursuing. That is certainly one approach. However, we believe that it perpetuates the very leadership styles we are protesting against, since it is about making power out of ideas and converting these ideas into dogmas that are then used to exploit and control others and to create division and competition rather than unity and collaboration.

In contrast, we are not interested in whether this model is right or wrong, but simply whether it is effective in practice. Do these ideas work in the "nitty-gritty" of day-to-day business life? We are primarily business coaches, not academics, and we speak as practitioners, not as theorists. On the eve of the interdependent era, we present these ideas to you as fuel for a conversation, as an evolving, emerging stream of consciousness that will change and flex as it moves into the world, as many hands make light work of it. If it has made you think a little deeper and little broader and if it has prompted more questions than given you answers, then we will feel that our job has been done.

EXERCISE

The prisoner's dilemma is a game developed by mathematician Albert W. Tucker in 1950. It neatly demonstrates in practice the challenges of shifting from the independent age of competition to the interdependent age of cooperation.

Imagine the following hypothetical situation. You and your partner in crime have been arrested for two robberies. The police are interrogating you both in separate cells. They have substantial evidence placing you at the scene of the crime of the first, less serious robbery, but they do not have sufficient evidence placing you at the second, more serious robbery. They have made a proposal to you: implicate your partner in the second robbery and you can get off with just probation. You know that your partner is being interrogated as well and that she may break. If she does, you could go to jail for a very long time.

Here are the consequences. If both you and your partner remain silent (cooperate with one another), you will both face light sentences of a year in jail each. If you both implicate one another (compete with each other), you will both face a long jail sentence of 10 years each. If you cooperate and your partner defects, then you will face an even longer sentence of 20 years and she will get probation. Finally, if you implicate your partner and she keeps quiet, then she will face 20 years and you will get probation. What do you do in such a situation? Would it matter whether you will encounter your partner again?

There is only one rational way to play this game: always defect (compete). If you think your opponent will cooperate, then you can get a higher score by choosing to defect. If you think your opponent will defect, the best you can do is also to defect. Yet, and this is the dilemma, if you had both cooperated, each of you would have done better.

The deeper FACTS

The prisoner's dilemma has been a staple of economic and human behavior studies for the past half-century. Cooperation would be in the best interests of both parties together, but individuals are tempted to defect because that leads to a better outcome for the individual no matter what the other player does. In a team context, the following exercise, which is a variation of the prisoner's dilemma, helps participants see how different strategies can solve competitive situations through collaboration. It supports the strengthening of teams.

Step 1: Participants are divided into two equal groups, A and B. The groups cannot communicate with each other except when specifically advised by the instructor (see Step 3). The groups are instructed that they can play the RED or the BLUE strategy. The words RED and BLUE are written on cards and each team gets one of each. They are told that the objective of the exercise is to get maximum points. The scoring is as follows:

- ❑ Both teams choose red: both score 2 points
- ❑ Both teams choose blue: both score 1 point
- ❑ One chooses blue and the other chooses red: blue gets 3 points and red 0 points

Step 2: In each round, the groups discuss among themselves whether they will play the RED or the BLUE strategy. After a sign from the instructor, each team holds up the card they have agreed on.

Step 3: After one round the scores are recorded for each team. The game is played over 10 rounds. After round 5, the teams can meet to negotiate (optional).

Step 4: After round 10, the final score is counted and a debriefing is held.

Comment: There are different scenarios for the outcome of this game. At the beginning, both teams may decide to choose red to maximize scoring, until one group decides blue. In the next phase, teams might try to trust each other and both play red until one group tries blue. The maximum an individual team can get is 30 points, if the other gets 0. The maximum aggregate score of both groups is 40, if both play red each time.

Conclusion

Throughout this book each chapter has been preceded by a phrase from the Tao Te Ching. The Tao Te Ching (translated as "The Great Way of Integrity") is an ancient collection of poetry written around the sixth century BC by a Chinese sage known as Lao Tzu. It consists of 81 verses that muse on topics such as war, nature, leadership, harmony, and personal development. Together the verses summarize the wisdom of the Chinese philosophy of Daoism. Central to Daoism are the concepts of yin and yang, as often represented by this famous symbol:

According to Daoism, yin and yang are two opposing energies in the world that wax and wane and represent the relative nature of all earthly things. In the symbol, the black represents the energy of yin, characterized by the qualities of dark, female, night, cold, soft, pull, and so on. The white represents the energy of yang, characterized by the qualities of light, male, day, hot, hard, push, and so on. As day always turns to night, yin and yang are always in constant transformation. Within the yin is always contained the seed of yang, as represented by the white dot. Likewise, within the yang is contained the seed of yin, as represented by the black dot. At the interface between yin and yang lies creative potential, the balancing point at which the two energies are in harmony and create the conditions for new forms to emerge into the world.

Using this metaphor, we can see that the first section of this book charts the history and status of coaching in business, revealing a predominantly yin activity that was born in a yang environment; that is, a soft presence that grew within a hard, booming business world. Yin skills such as listening, asking questions, building rapport, and a nondirective ethos were a great antidote to the yang bias of telling, directing, analyzing, and controlling. As coaching has grown, this core of yin energy has expanded and blossomed, creating many positive impacts as it intermingles with its yang environment.

Yet whenever yin energy expands, it inevitably sows the seed of the white dot of yang energy within its midst. As Chapter 3 developed the core principles of the FACTS coaching approach, we sensed this change of energy as the yang principles of "build the contract, honor the contract" and "speak your truth, face the facts" were revealed. This focus became clearer as the yang skills of challenging feedback, accountability, courageous goals, and tension were outlined as the underlying components of the FACTS model. In this context, yin represents the support axis of the support/challenge matrix and yang the challenge axis.

In a mirror image of this shift, the world of business shows signs of reaching the peak of its yang epoch. There is continual and growing pressure to appoint more female leaders into senior positions at large companies. There is an ongoing global backlash against leaders who have abused power and privilege through assuming dictatorial positions. There is a growing tide of pressure from diverse stakeholders to broaden the vision of the business world to embrace sustainable practices with regard to the environment, energy, and waste. In a predominantly yang-dominated business world one can understand how a yin-dominated coaching style grew up to provide a contrast and to complement this bias. However, if now the yin is slowly rising in the business environment, the coaching challenge is to sense this shift and adapt our stance to respond quickly and effectively with yang interventions as and when circumstances dictate.

Chapter 7 reminded us that tension can be a constructive, transformative energy if we work with it consciously as part of our coaching approach. Using the yin/yang metaphor, tension can be pictured as the interface between yin and yang: the curling "S" shape that divides the earlier symbol. As this interface is approached, the tension increases to an optimum in line with the Yerkes–Dodson law. If a coach or leader can hold the tension and so work at the edge, at the interface of these two energies, then a point of creative potential exists. There is a balancing point at which yin and yang come into harmony. Picture a courageous tightrope walker traversing a deep gorge, tense yet lightly gripping the balancing bar and proceeding with deliberate steadiness toward a unique goal. This is our image of the FACTS coach working with individuals and teams and holding to the transformative edge of the yin/yang balance—the point at which transformation spontaneously takes place.

Yang is not more important or more critical than yin; this is not a battle for supremacy of these equally valid approaches. It is, in contrast, a continual pursuit of harmony and balance in these skills. Clearly, this book has focused on the yang, FACTS component of challenging coaching. This is because we believe that this is the fresh, emerging energy in a young, yin-dominated profession, the edge where potential can be explored to greatest effect. However, in no way is this focus intended to denigrate or subsume the solid and essential foundation of supportive yin coaching skills, which remain a core component of a holistic coaching presence.

As practitioners, the key is to develop confident, skillful access to the full range of yin and yang coaching principles, skills, and techniques. We must seek not to be self-constrained in working only in one dimension of the support/challenge dynamic, the dimension that suits our own needs and preferences rather than those of the organization we are working with. To be so constrained does not serve our clients or the people we lead, who may benefit at different stages in their development and performance from all the shades of the yin/yang spectrum of coaching. The contrast itself is often the most catalytic key for the unlocking of full potential. Our prime responsibility is to seek our own development "edge" and in so doing to inspire others to do likewise through our personal example—to "be the change we want to see in the world."

Chapter 8, with its focus on systems thinking, highlighted how the organizational world is made up of many subsystems, each with its yin and yang components. We realize that the earlier yin/yang diagram is a simplification of reality that belongs to the person-centered ideology, a pure focus on one individual's own energetic cycle. In contrast, the equivalent systems-centered diagram would look more like this:

This diagram reveals a chaotic pattern of subsystems, each influencing the other to generate myriad different possibilities. The coach enters this complexity armed with a foundation of yin, supporting skills, yet also with the ability to adopt a challenging, yang stance as and when appropriate to the environment. They intuitively gauge the right balance that will create the most profound, system-wide impact depending on the personalities, team profile, organizational and country culture in which they are operating at that precise moment. This is an artistic dance rather than a scientific equation.

Today, you may be working with a yin individual in a yang organizational culture. In this scenario, you might initially pace the coachee with a supportive, yin style of coaching to build rapport and trust. Later, a challenging, yang style using FACTS skills could be introduced to mirror the coachee's organizational environment and to ensure that the coaching stays aligned to the current reality of the situation. Tomorrow, you may be working with a yang individual in a yin organizational culture and the starting situation will be reversed. In this scenario, it is likely that initial rapport and credibility will be built using a challenging, yang style. As the coaching relationship matures and deepens, a supportive, yin style can be introduced to soften the engagement and create empathy with the wider organizational context. In both scenarios there are many possible combinations and permutations in which the coach discerns how and when to balance the more challenging skills of the FACTS coaching model dynamically with other established models and techniques as part of a flexible, integrated approach.

In general, FACTS coaching will be most useful for coaches who are already adept at building supportive, high-trust relationships, but who are seeking a means to "kick on" and raise their game to the next level in order to accelerate the business impact of their work. The diagram below sums up this cycle, in which the initial focus when working with others is often to build trust and respect using primarily the yin, supportive skills of the coaching style armed with models such as GROW. Once this has been achieved then, rather than risk a plateau of performance, the coach changes gear and shifts to the challenging, FACTS end of the spectrum to leverage the trusted relationship and stretch for higher goals. Crucially, this is not done at the expense of trust and respect, but as means of building on them. The net effect is to accelerate the delivery of sustainable bottom-line impacts and unlock a new level of potential.

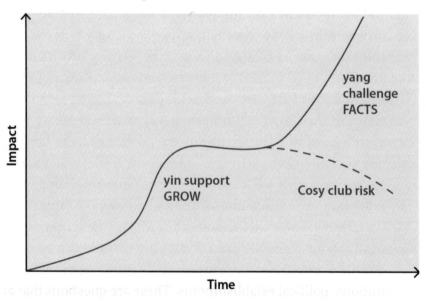

The idea of the leader as "player-coach" was introduced in Chapter 9. A FACTS style of coaching is relevant for leaders and managers as well as professional coaches. The practical goal is that a leader can still combine their doing skills with their managing skills and use the FACTS coaching approach in 10-minute bursts when facing the whole range of daily conversations with team members, bosses, peers, and clients. This is itself a complex nest of systems and can feel as chaotic as the earlier diagram of overlapping yin and yang symbols. The player-coach moves rapidly and dynamically from subsystem to subsystem using FACTS skills to intervene precisely where they can have the most impact, trusting that the ripples of such interventions will flow out from their conversations like a pebble dropped into a pond. In many ways this is an appeal to focus on conversations and trust that the bigger picture will look after itself if this attention to detail is applied with the right intention and spirit.

In Chapter 10, we explored the deeper FACTS, looking beyond the world of business to the broader trends in society at large. We explored the possibility that the rising yin of the business world is symptomatic of global trends, particularly the yearning for freedom that seems pervasive across societies regardless of culture and history. Freedom is a yin word, responsibility is yang. To speak of yang when the world wishes to embrace yin is to risk ridicule and criticism and to provoke easy misunderstandings. It also provides a temptation to step into dogma and absolute moral statements that polarize opinion in a way that, while often dramatic and entertaining, does not focus on the most effective, practical, day-to-day behavior of coaches. This chapter raises questions about the application of the FACTS coaching approach outside the world of business: in families, schools, sport, religious institutions, political establishments. These are questions that are outside the scope of this book, yet we hope that others, who are experts in those fields, may be provoked to explore the relevance of this thinking in such domains.

The vision of an interdependent culture presented in Chapter 10 is one in which yin and yang energies intertwine and partner to create new possibilities. It represents a mature acceptance of the reality of a diverse, dualistic, complex world and a letting go of the denial of this complexity by the imposition of simplistic, absolute conclusions. It may sound grandiose to suggest that a simple coaching approach and mindset may be one small part of the facilitation of such a shift but, as the chapter points out in its closing paragraphs, change only happens one conversation at a time. It is the quality of our conversations not the power of our intellects that will ultimately determine the future we create.

Regardless of the arena in which it is practiced, underlying the FACTS approach is one word: courage. It is about the courage to have the conversation that is being avoided, to speak the truth that is being ignored, and to name the unfulfilling reality that is being tolerated. It is about the courage to step into the black when all are in the white, or to step into the white when all are in the black; to enter the ZOUD with the intent to seek the best interests of the wider whole, the organizational system itself. Doing this can create a feeling of utter isolation, yet it also represents an act of intense personal leadership within which lies the scope for a deep fulfillment of purpose and meaning.

Beyond the philosophy of yin and yang, the effectiveness of the FACTS approach will ultimately be measured through sustainable bottom-line improvements in the performance of individuals, teams, and organizations. Whatever the stage of the economic cycle, there are always challenging situations that are triggered by the growth, sustainability, and decline of companies. In all phases, leaders need to challenge and leaders need to be challenged. We hope that the philosophies and practical skills detailed in this book will enable the ZOUD to be entered more often and with higher confidence on behalf of the greater good.

As we bring this book to a close, it seems apt to leave the final words to our ancient friend Lao Tzu. If he were alive today, we hope that he would approve of the FACTS approach and even be persuaded to attend one of our masterclasses as a guest speaker!

It would give him the opportunity to declare that there is really nothing new under the sun; he had this worked out 2,600 years ago, if only we had been listening. Or in his own words:

> *Countless words count less than the silent balance between yin and yang. (Tao Te Ching, Verse 5)*

Bibliography

Bateson, Gregory (2000) *Steps to an Ecology of Mind: Collected Essays in Anthropology, Psychiatry, Evolution and Epistemology.* University of Chicago Press.

Beattie, Melody (1989) *Codependent No More: How to Stop Controlling Others and Start Caring for Yourself.* Hazelden Information & Educational Services.

Bowman, Cliff (1995) Strategy workshops and top-team commitment to strategic change. *Journal of Managerial Psychology* 10(8): 4–12.

Campbell, Joseph (1993) *The Hero with a Thousand Faces.* Fontana.

Collins, James C and Porras, Jerry I (1997) *Built to Last: Successful Habits of Visionary Companies.* HarperBusiness.

Covey, Stephen R (2004) *The 7 Habits of Highly Effective People: Powerful Lessons in Personal Change.* Simon and Schuster.

Daloz, Laurent (1986) *Effective Teaching and Mentoring.* Jossey-Bass.

Dienstbier, Richard A (1989) Arousal and physiological toughness: Implications for mental and physical health. *Psychological Review* 96(1): 84–100.

Egan, George (1982) *The Skilled Helper: A Problem-Management Approach to Helping.* Brooks/Cole.

Hofstede, Geert (2003) *Culture's Consequences: Comparing Values, Behaviors, Institutions and Organizations Across Nations.* Sage.

Jackson, Paul Z and McKergow, Mark (2008) *The Solutions Focus: Making Coaching & Change SIMPLE*, 2nd edn. Nicholas Brealey Publishing.

Jung, CG (1991) *The Archetypes and the Collective Unconscious.* Routledge.

Kuhn, Lesley (2009) *Adventures in Complexity: For Organizations Near the Edge of Chaos.* Triarchy Press.

Lao Tzu (2002) *Tao Te Ching*. Watkins Publishing.

Lorenz, Edward (1998) *The Essence of Chaos*. Routledge.

Ludeman, Kate and Erlandson, Eddie (2004) Coaching the alpha male. *Harvard Business Review* May.

Maslow, Abraham H (2011) *Toward a Psychology of Being*. Wilder Publications.

Meadows, Donella H (2009) *Thinking in Systems: A Primer*. Routledge.

Pang-Jeng Lo, Benjamin, Inn, Martin, and Amacker, Robert (1982) *The Essence of T'ai Chi Ch'uan: The Literary Tradition*. North Atlantic Books.

Patton, Bruce, Stone, Douglas, and Heen, Sheila (2000) *Difficult Conversations: How to Discuss What Matters Most*. Penguin.

Plotkin, Bill (2008) *Nature and the Human Soul: Cultivating Wholeness in a Fragmented World*. New World Library.

Podsakoff, Nathan P, LePine, Jeffrey A, and LePine, Marice A. (2007) Differential challenge stressor-hindrance stressor relationships with job attitudes, turnover intentions, turnover, and withdrawal behavior: A meta-analysis. *Journal of Applied Psychology* 92(2): 438–54.

Rogers, CR (1957) The necessary and sufficient conditions of therapeutic personality change. *Journal of Consulting Psychology* 21(2): 95–103.

Scott, Susan (2003) *Fierce Conversations: Achieving Success in Work and in Life, One Conversation at a Time*. Piatkus.

Senge, Peter M (1994) *The Fifth Discipline: The Art and Practice of the Learning Organization*. Bantam Doubleday Dell.

Yerkes, Robert M and Dodson, John D (1908) The relation of strength of stimulus to rapidity of habit-formation. *Journal of Comparative Neurology and Psychology* 18: 459–82.

Whitmore, Sir John (1997) *Need, Greed or Freedom: Business Changes and Personal Choices*. Element.

Whitmore, Sir John (2009) *Coaching for Performance: GROWing Human Potential and Purpose. The Principles and Practice of Coaching Leadership*, 4th edn. Nicholas Brealey Publishing.

Whitworth, Laura, Kimsey-House, Henry, Kimsey-House, Karen, and Sandahl, Phil (2011) *Co-Active Coaching: New Skills for Coaching People Toward Success in Work and Life*, 3rd edn. Nicholas Brealey Publishing.

Index

About the authors

John Blakey is a coach to board-level leaders around the globe, having worked in the US, UK, Australia, Holland, Sweden, Norway, Belgium, Portugal, Czech Republic, Malaysia, India, France, and Germany in recent years. In his corporate career he was international managing director at Logica plc and later its director of coaching, the first such role in a FTSE250 organization. In the 1990s he was consulting director of Team121 Ltd, one of the fastest-growing private companies in the UK. He has an MSc in Information Systems and an MBA from Aston Business School, and features regularly as a conference speaker and writer on the topics of executive coaching, organizational change, and business growth. His work draws on a broad spectrum of influences including his expertise in t'ai chi, his work with Olympic athletes and their coaches, his Christian faith, and his passion for systems thinking. Visit www.johnblakey.co.uk for more information about John.

Ian Day is a coach, facilitator, and speaker working at board level for large international clients. Ian graduated with a degree in psychology and spent over 20 years in human resource and development roles in a variety of large organizations within the leisure and tourism, healthcare and utilities sectors, including head of talent for an international FTSE100 group, responsible for groupwide talent management, leadership development, executive coaching, and performance management. In this role Ian was coached, which was an inspiring turning point in his life and led him to study for an advanced diploma in coaching and mentoring, a certificate in counseling, and to his current work as a leadership consultant. Ian's interest in psychology has never left him as he applies models and theories in his work with individuals and teams, frequently using psychometric personality profiles to create within clients the awareness and energy to change. Ian believes that everyone has greatness within themselves, and he works to release this potential by applying the model and skills of FACTS coaching.™ Visit www.FACTScoaching.com for more information about Ian.

For additional information and resources and to find out more, visit www.challengingcoaching.co.uk